TIME AND THE CALENDARS

THE MEXICAN CALENDAR STONE, in Mexico City, a twenty-ton
monolith carved early in the 16th century AD, symbolizes many of the
Aztecs' conceptions of Time and the Cosmos. The face in the centre
represents the present Sun and the four rectangles around it represent
the four previous eras in which the whole Cosmos was successively
created and destroyed. The surrounding circle of twenty rectangles give
the names of the days in the so-called 'month'. Beyond that there are
symbols of the day and of the night, the year and much else besides.

W. M. O'NEIL / TIME AND THE CALENDARS

SYDNEY
UNIVERSITY
PRESS

SYDNEY UNIVERSITY PRESS

Press Building, University of Sydney

NORTH AND SOUTH AMERICA
International Scholarly Book Services, Inc., Portland, Oregon

National Library of Australia Cataloguing-in-Publication data

O'Neil, William Matthew
    Time and the calendars/ [by] W. M. O'Neil.—Sydney:
Sydney University Press, 1975.
    Index.
    Bibliography.
    ISBN 0 424 00003 2.

    1. Calendar—History.   I. Title.

529.3

First published 1975
© W. M. O'Neil 1975

This book is funded by money from
THE ELEANOR SOPHIA WOOD BEQUEST

Printed in Australia by Macarthur Press, Parramatta

CONTENTS

Frontispiece
The Mexican Calendar Stone in Mexico City

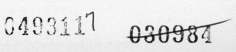

LIST OF FIGURES

LIST OF TABLES

PREFACE

Time, at least conceptually, flows on continuously and uniformly. Man, however, has constructed numerous calendars and time-pieces in order to mark off its passage in long and short units to suit his various needs. These needs were at first entirely practical—when to plough, sow and harvest, when to propitiate the gods so that rains or floods or a good crop would be ensured or that evils of one kind or another would be warded off. Later he needed for intellectual reasons to understand, to account for and to improve the time measures he used; thus astronomy developed.

Several rather obvious naturally-recurring events of an astronomical sort were available for time-reckoning. Amongst these were the day (made up of a period of daylight and a period of night), the lunar month marked out by the cycle of phases of the Moon and the solar year marked out by the apparent motion of the Sun west to east among the fixed stars which could be seen just before sunrise and just after sunset and between limiting points north (summer) and south (winter) in the sky. These three natural periods unfortunately were incommensurable, the month being about 29.53 days on average and the year in ancient times about 365.243 days or about 12.33 months. Those calendar-makers who emphasized the months either ignored the year (producing a lunar calendar) or added a thirteenth month every now and then in order to get the year right on average (producing a luni-solar calendar). Those who emphasized the year ignored the phases of the Moon though they often had schematic months of 29, 30 or 31 days, so producing a solar calendar.

Of course for some purposes a day, even a day in the sense of the period of daylight, or a night, is too coarse a unit of time. So man began to look for or to invent clocks which would enable him to subdivide the day. Certain stars chosen because they were about $10°$ apart in celestial longitude were used in Egypt and perhaps in Babylonia to divide the night and sun-dials were developed to divide the period of sunlight. Then came the water-clock, called by the Greeks *clepsydra*, the water-stealer, as it leaked water to mark the hours. Later came mechanical clocks, controlled first by leaking water, then by a pendulum and later by the escapement-wheel mechanism. We now have atomic clocks. The units used in these various clocks were arbitrary, dividing the day into twelfths, twenty-fourths, sixtieths or hundredths, each as a rule with further fractions. The month readily divided naturally into halves, new Moon to full Moon and next new Moon, the periods being 14 or 15 days, or into quarters, new Moon to first half Moon to full Moon to second half Moon to next new Moon, periods of about 7 days (sometimes 8 in rounded days). These quarter-months may have produced our arbitrary 7-day week. Another favoured division of the month was into thirds of about 10 days, a waxing third, a middle third and a waning third; this may have been related to use of the Egyptian thirty-six stars, the decans, to mark the 'hours' of the night as this schema slipped forward one star in the series every 10 days. The solar year for those living north of the tropics may have seemed clearly enough divided into four seasons later regarded as being marked off by the equinoxes (when the Sun was crossing the Celestial Equator in spring and autumn) and by the solstices (when the Sun reached its most northern and most southern altitudes in summer and winter respectively). The intervals between equinoxes and solstices are not quite equal but some early calendar-makers assumed that they were, for the differences amount to only a few days and the precise date of an equinox or solstice is not easy to determine within a day or two. Some calendar-makers, especially those in the tropics or near-tropics were more impressed by local meteorological conditions than by the equinoxes and solstices, thus the ancient Egyptians had 3 seasons each of 4 months and the Indians in Vedic times had 6 seasons each of 2 months.

The following pages set out to give an account of the various major calendars on the basis of an account first of the guiding recurring astronomical events and second of the various arbitrary subdivisions of the periods of time so provided. This has been done many times in the past. Among the best efforts I have encountered are the article by Fotheringham in *The Nautical Almanac for the Year* 1931 (and repeated in several later editions of that reference work) and the composite articles on calendars in *The Encyclopaedia of Religion and Ethics*, edited by Hastings (1910) and in *The Encyclopaedia Britannica* (1973 edn). All suffer from some brevity, the two encyclo-paedia articles suffer from multi-authorship resulting in some failure of cross comparison, and all suffer to varying degrees from failure to include the results of more recent scholarship which has been voluminous in the case of several major calendars and which has often post-dated the writing of these useful general articles. There are also several small books produced in the last fifty years examining past calendrical practices and arguing reformation of them. I have located five such works in the bibliographies available to me but have been able to study only three of them. These three are interesting and informative but to my mind they suffer several defects. First, they are unduly concerned with the deficiencies of all past calendars and with the way their proposed reformed calendar can overcome these deficiencies. Second, they are loose in their specification of basic astronomical periods; perhaps I have been unduly obsessional in specifying them to many decimal places of a day. Third, they are generally careless in citing their historical references. I have tried to do better by citing important secondary sources for almost everything I claim, secondary sources in which reference to the primary sources is made.

My intention has not been to propose reforms of our irrational calendar. It has been to give an account of the attempts to produce workable calendars in what is perhaps an impossible situation. This account is not aimed at experts but instead at the general reader and at students in various fields who need to understand the calendars which they encounter in the course of their studies. Hence, my citation of so many basic scholars reporting their findings in journal and in monographic publications.

I have been severely limited by my own linguistic deficiencies. I have had mainly to rely on what is available in English, supplemented by what I can slowly read and partially understand in French and in German. At times I have been forced back into Latin which I can understand even less well, and I have done my best to understand some words in Greek, Sumerian, Akkadian and Sanskrit, mainly by use of transliterations which I have looked up in dictionaries. My use of Chinese and Meso-American words is completely pretentious.

A large number of friends, acquaintances and colleagues have been of great help to me. Several astronomer friends have helped me find or understand some quantity which I have used. My numerous friends expert in various languages have helped me in the interpretation of some passage in a foreign language which puzzled me or left me uncertain or drew my attention to some recent or less recent publication which might help me. I owe a special debt to Professor Ho Peng-yoke, until recently of the University of Malaysia, who during his brief visit to the University of Sydney spent time talking to me and after it in digging out for me information I needed. Dr Noel Weeks provided me with a platform from which I might jump, possibly into the dark (in which case it is entirely my own fault), into some understanding of the Babylonian names of the zodiacal constellations and the Signs of the Zodiac. Other friends have supplied me with day-names in various languages and explained their meanings to me. I also owe a debt to all of those who have ensured that so many of the books and periodicals I have used are in the Fisher Library of the University of Sydney and to those members of the staff of that Library but especially Miss Gladys Bennett who so diligently obtained for me through inter-library loan the other materials which I needed. Mr Ian Langham read the near final version of the book and made many helpful suggestions.

I have other debts which must be acknowledged. First to Miss Dorothy O'Connor who typed and retyped ungrudgingly so much of my many-times revised manuscript, to Miss Sheina Lambert who typed, during Miss O'Connor's absence, a substantial part of the penultimate manuscript and to Miss Nancy Smith and Miss Maureen McGowan who retyped many pages in the final version. Second, and above all, to my wife who not only put up with my obsession with time and the calendars, to the neglect of other things which she knew I should be doing, but who also read the whole thing and advised me on how I might improve my spelling, punctuation and expression.

What is reported in the pages which follow is in many ways the result of a personal quest based mainly on the study of second-hand sources. I was trying in this quest to satisfy some personal curiosities. I recognize that in reporting my conclusions I often rely on my hunches not fully supported by solid evidence. Hence I have often used the first personal pronoun to an extent which I have been told may irritate many of my readers.

At the end of the self-imposed task I recognize how unequal I was to it. I hope, nevertheless, that those who may read what I have written may be stimulated enough and be given clues enough to work out a better book for themselves.

The University of Sydney   W. M. O'NEIL
February 1975

1/SOME FEATURES OF OUR CALENDAR AND THEIR ORIGINS

Having just consulted my watch and my diary, I know that it is now 8.15 p.m., Friday, 2 February AD 1973. My watch read 7.15 but I remembered that it was set an hour early on Summer Time, and that in any case the 8.15 I just mentioned is only Eastern Australian Standard Time which runs 2 hours later than mean time at the International Date Line and 10 hours earlier than Greenwich Mean Time. Though I shall be forced before long to consider a wider world let me begin by considering only what applies to my circumscribed nest in Sydney.

I have from my watch, my diary and a certain framework of information provided by my memory or by references which I can consult should my memory fail, at least five data locating for me where I am in the passage of time. I shall take the five in reverse order. I have:

(i) A year numbered in the Christian Era deemed to have begun at about the time of the birth of Christ. From memory I know that ordinary years in our calendar consist of 365 days and that leap years consist of 366 days, the latter being years when February has a twenty-ninth day. I also remember the Julian rule that every fourth year is a leap year and the Gregorian correction that centurial years such as AD 1700, 1800 and 1900 not divisible without remainder by 400 are not leap years.

(ii) A named month which my memory informs me is the second in a cycle of twelve, running January, February, March, ..., December.

(iii) An ordinally numbered day in the month. I also remember the jingle 'Thirty days hath September, April, June and November, all the rest have thirty-one, except February etc.' Thus putting (i), (ii) and (iii) together, I can deduce that this February in which I am now has twenty-six more whole days to run.

(iv) A named day in a week which my memory tells me runs Sunday, Monday, Tuesday, Wednesday, Thursday, Friday and Saturday.

1

Thus I can recognize that today is the sixth day of a 7-day week.

(v) A time within the day stated in terms of hours and minutes. Strictly speaking my watch indirectly informs me only that it is 8.15. My memory, aided perhaps by the perceived state of the natural light, supplies the 'p.m.'; from this I infer that twenty and a quarter hours have expired from the last midnight when the day was deemed to begin and that another three and three-quarter hours have to expire before the next midnight when the day will be deemed to end. That is, I recognize that the hour-hand of my watch, were it set to Eastern Australian Standard Time, would be making its second circuit since it was on twelve when the day began and that the minute-hand would have made one-quarter of its twenty-first circuit. The first hour-hand's circuit is called a.m. from *ante meridiem* and the second p.m. from *post meridiem*. The *meridiem* or middle of the day is related to the meridian, an imaginary line running north-south in the sky through the zenith, a point immediately overhead for a given observer. The Sun crosses the meridian at about 12 noon but, as we shall see, not usually exactly so. When the Sun is east of the meridian, apart from the slight variation just mentioned, the hours are *ante meridiem*; when it is west of the meridian, the hours are *post meridiem*. Though we count the hours and minutes forward from 12 noon, the approximate time of the solar meridian crossing, we do not count them backwards from 12 noon as the expression 11.30 *ante meridiem* might suggest.

Some of this information derived from watch; diary and memory (aided by reference sources) is expressed in terms related to observable recurring astronomical events, but much is expressed in terms that are conventional, some being quite arbitrary. Let me illustrate this claim first by some consideration of the day, its subdivision into hours and minutes and its location within the week.

I shall use the term day, as most calendar-makers do, to mean some combination of daylight (called 'day' in ordinary English usage) and of night, i.e., (i) when the Sun, directly as in sunlight or indirectly as in the two twilight periods, illuminates the Earth, and (ii) when the Sun does not so illuminate the Earth and when the stars can be seen. Daylight and night succeed each other primarily as a result of the Earth's rotation around its axis but the duration of the combined periods is also a result of the Earth's revolution around the Sun. About 23 hours 56 minutes elapse between successive meridian crossings of some fixed star. This is the period of the Earth's rotation around its axis; it is almost constant but not quite. Because the Earth also revolves around the Sun in a little less than 365.25 days, the Sun appears to be moving eastward among the fixed stars by an average of almost $0.99°$ of angle per day. As a consequence the Sun crosses the meridian on average at intervals about 4 minutes longer than those for stellar meridian crossings, that is on average at intervals of 24 hours. All that has been said in this paragraph is based on astronomical facts, approximately stated though they be.

There is still the issue of when the day should be deemed to begin. There are three readily observable astronomical events involving the Sun which we may use for this purpose. First, sunrise (or as a related alternative the beginning of the period before sunrise usually called dawn or the morning twilight when the Sun's indirect light fades out the stars). Second, the midday solar meridian crossing. Third, sunset (or as a related alternative the end of the period of evening twilight when the stars shine forth again). The first (perhaps dawn rather than sunrise) was favoured by the ancient Egyptians and the third (sunset) by the ancient Babylonians and, possibly following them, by the Greeks and Jews. Later Hellenistic astronomers such as Ptolemy (*circa* second century AD) favoured the solar meridian crossing. A more abstract, or computed, start of the day is midway through the night which may be estimated in various ways. Hipparchos, perhaps the greatest Hellenistic astronomer (*circa* second century BC), the Romans (for some purposes) and the Chinese from an early stage favoured starting the day at midnight as we do.

To determine midnight we need a clock of some sort. A star may be used on a given occasion for this purpose. Imagine a given star rising due east at about sunset in spring or autumn; at about midnight it will have its meridian crossing. Though this may hold for that star on one night, on the next it will make its meridian crossing about 4 minutes early for reasons already given. After ten nights from the original occasion when it made its meridian crossing at midnight it will run 40 minutes early. The ancient Egyptians quite early selected stars about $10°$ in longitude apart to act as 'hour-hands' of shifting value for successive periods of 10 days. In the mid-second millennium BC at the latest the Egyptians had devised a water-clock which leaked at near constant rate the water with which it was filled and so indicated by the height of the water the hours of the night. Either they or the Babylonians, though there are claims for the Greeks, may be credited

3

with the invention of a sun-dial for indicating the hours of the sunlight period more accurately than could be established merely by looking to see where the Sun was in the sky. Though we thus have several natural or calculated markers from which to begin the day, it is a matter of convention as to which of the several markers we choose.

The selection of 24 hours as the subdivision of the day is quite arbitrary. The Chinese for example used twelve sub-units of the day and the Hindus came to use 60 sub-units. Though the day, wherever we begin and end it, is about the same length as a result of certain recurrent astronomical events, no natural event breaks the day, rough measured though it be, into twelfths, twenty-fourths, sixtieths or any other fractions. One may as readily choose one fraction as another. After a time the ancient Egyptians settled down into dividing daylight (I suspect sunlight plus the two twilights) into twelfths and night into twelfths. At Memphis which is about 30°N. in terrestrial latitude there are about 16 hours and 45 minutes (by the clock) of daylight, sunlight plus bordering twilights, in mid-summer and about 11 hours and 2 minutes in mid-winter. Thus, dividing daylight into twelfths will yield long daylight 'hours' in summer and short daylight 'hours' in winter. It follows that the summer night 'hours' will be short and the winter night 'hours' long. These unequal 'hours' were called by the Greeks and the Romans 'temporal hours'. The Babylonians, at an early stage, used twelve equal fractions of the day measured from sunset to sunset but later they also seem to have adopted the Egyptian scheme of twenty-four 'temporal hours' but with a difference. They had twelve 'hours' from sunset to sunrise and twelve from sunrise to sunset. In spring and autumn, at the equinoxes, these Babylonian 'temporal hours' were equal for both night and sunlight and were 60 of our minutes. In the late second century BC Hipparchos suggested that these uniform equinoctial hours be adopted as standard hours (no doubt measured by a clock). It was he, as already reported, who decided to count these standard hours of the day, which we still use in slightly modified form, from midnight.

The Egyptians and the Babylonians had different number systems. The Egyptians had a decimal system for whole numbers, that is digits, tens, hundreds, thousands, etc. but for fractions, except for one fraction, namely two-thirds, used in certain calculations, they used unit fractions, that is one-half, one-third, one-quarter, one-fifth, one-sixth, etc. To state three-quarters or .75, the Egyptians wrote in effect (one-half + one-quarter); to state 19/20 or .95 they wrote in effect (one-half + one-quarter + one-fifth). The Babylonians had a sex-agesimal system both for whole numbers and for fractions. Further the Babylonian notation was completely positional. We write 947 to indicate 9 hundreds, 4 tens and 7 digits, and 947.31 to indicate 9 hundreds, 4 tens, 7 digits, 3 tenths and 1 hundredth. The Romans wrote 947 as *CMXLVII* meaning (a hundred less than a thousand) *plus* (ten less than fifty) *plus* five *plus* two digits. In a way this Roman number system is decimal with a quinquagesimal underlay: digits (*I*), fives (*V*), tens (*X*), fifties (*L*), hundreds (*C*), five hundreds (*D*), thousands (*M*). Except that the larger values were written first, the numerals are not positional. Putting a lower numeral (but rarely more than one) in front of a higher one indicated a shortfall by the amount of the former from the latter, thus *CM* is a hundred less than a thousand, *XL* is ten less than fifty and *IX* is one less than ten. A higher numeral followed by a lower numeral signified that the latter was added to the former. A repeated numeral meant a multiple of the numeral, thus *XXX* meant 3 tens or 30, *XXXI* meant 31 whereas *XXIX* meant 29. Earlier the Romans had decimal fractions, each with their symbol, for units of length, area, weight and money. Later they adopted duodecimal fractions. In neither system were there fractions of fractions. They also referred to fractions in words, for example 'a third part'. None of these systems was amenable to ready arithmetic manipulation.

The Babylonians could write quite large whole numbers and quite fine fractions in their sexagesimal positional number system. Using our numerals, commas to mark off positions and a semi-colon to indicate the beginning of a fraction (all conventions borrowed from Neugebauer, 1969, pp. 31 ff). I shall write our 947.31 in something like their manner, namely 15,47; 18,36 meaning 15 sixties, 47 digits, 18 sixtieths and 36/3,600ths. Such a system of numerals was amenable to ready arithmetical operations.

If my authorities have not misled me into my belief that at least late Babylonians were using the 24 temporal hour division of the day, I suggest that Hipparchos based his standard hours on the Babylonian temporal hours at the equinoxes rather than the Egyptian for he calculated them from sunset to sunrise and from sunrise to sunset and not from beginning of morning twilight to end of evening twilight and from end of evening twilight to beginning of morning twilight. Further he went on to divide them into Babylonian sexagesimal fractions. Later in Latin the first or 1/60th fraction was referred to as *pars minuta* (small part), the second or 1/3,600th fraction as *pars secunda*, the third or 1/216,000th fraction as *pars tertia* and so on. Hence our minutes and seconds. Even Copernicus in the sixteenth century AD was using minutes, seconds, thirds, etc., that is, sexagesimal fractions of the hour and of the degree of angle. In more recent times we have come to stop the sexagesimal fractions at seconds for both time and angles and then resort to decimal fractions, that is tenths and hundredths of a second, milliseconds and nanoseconds. It is obvious that all of this is quite arbitrary.

The 7-day week is also arbitrary though it has some astronomical associations. Our day names Sunday, Monday, ..., Saturday, come quite directly from the early Imperial, possibly late Republican, Roman *Dies Solis*, *Dies Lunae*, *Dies Martis*, *Dies Mercurii*, *Dies Iouis*, *Dies Veneris* and *Dies Saturni*. These names identify each of the 7 days in the week with one of the 7 wanderers among the fixed stars known in antiquity, Sun (*Sol*), Moon (*Luna*), Mars, Mercury, Jupiter, Venus and Saturn. Our English names substitute some roughly analogous Teutonic gods for the Roman ones whose names were attached to the planets, Twia for Mars, Woden for Mercury, Thor for Jupiter and Frigga for Venus. These planetary names almost certainly have an astrological origin which has suggested to some that they are Babylonian. Though the concept may have been Babylonian, the naming is probably Hellenistic (see Neugebauer, 1969, pp. 169–70).

The Jews, at least since the Babylonian Exile have had a 7-day week. Only one, *Shabbat*, the day of rest and of religious observance, had a proper name; the others were simply First Day, Second Day and so on. Some Latin writers in early Imperial times identified the Jewish Sabbath with Saturn's day and went on to conclude that the jews were Saturn-worshippers.

There are suggestions that both the planetary week and the Jewish week had their origins in Babylonian conventions, (see Langdon, 1935, pp. 73 ff). In the early seventh century BC some records made in Assyria indicate that work was proscribed on the seventh, fourteenth, twenty-first and twenty-eighth days of the month. As the month concerned was strictly lunar, these days were approximately those of the first half Moon, the full Moon, the second half Moon and the disappearance of the Moon respectively. As Babylonian months had 29 and 30 days in rough alternation there were 1 or 2 days outside these 'weeks'.

When the early Christians adopted the Jewish continuous week they made the first day the Lord's Day, the one of greatest religious significance, as Christ's resurrection occurred on the day after the Jewish Sabbath following the Passover. The Passover celebrated the escape of the Jewish first born and the subsequent escape of the Jews from Egypt. It was held on the day of the full Moon after the Spring Equinox. At some fairly early date the Christians were using the planetary names of the days despite their almost certain astrological origin. Indeed by the early fourth century AD this planetary week seems to have been regarded as distinctively Christian.

Though our word 'month' is derived from 'Moon', we use months based on the Republican Roman months. Neither the Republican nor the later Julian months are more than vestiges of the synodic months, this is, the month embracing the phases of the Moon which is on average about 29.53 days. Babylonian, Greek and Chinese months were not only of 29 or 30 days (in rough alternation thus providing a good practical approximation to an average of 29.53 days), but also they were closely tied to the phases of the Moon. The Roman months, though perhaps at a very early date tied to the cycle of phases of the Moon, were later not so tied. They merely resembled the lunar months in duration. The same is true of the Egyptian 30-day months. The number of days in each of our months are those set by Julius Caesar when he reformed the earlier Roman calendar from what we now call 45 BC. Except for 2 months, July (instead of *Quintilis*) and August (instead of *Sextilis*) the month names are early Latin names.

We number the days in the month forward from the first day as did the Babylonians, the Jews, the Indians, the Chinese and many Greeks. The Romans, however, did not. They had three points in the month: the Kalends (the first day), the Nones (the fifth in most months but the seventh in four) and the Ides (the thirteenth in most months but the fifteenth in four). Days other than these were numbered backwards from them. As the February Nones occurred on the fifth day of that month our 4 February was the day before the February Nones, *pridie Nonas Februarias* and as a result of the Roman custom of inclusive counting, our 3 February was the third day before the Nones or *ante diem tertium Nonas Februarias*. In the Julian leap year the extra day in February was placed not at the end of the month as we place it but instead between the twenty-fourth and the normal twenty-fifth day. Both these days kept their usual designations (but see Samuel, 1972, p. 156), namely the sixth and fifth days before the March Kalends and the extra day became the second sixth day before the Kalends of March, or *ante diem bissextum Kalendas Martias*.

It is clear from the names, *December*, *November*, *October*, *September* and the earlier *Sextilis* and *Quintilis* (to state them in reverse order) that at some earlier date the Romans began the year in March (*Martius*). However, long before Julius' reform of the calendar, the first day of January was regarded as the first day of the year or New Year's Day. Julius preserved this convention. The decision as to when the year is deemed to begin is completely arbitrary. There are four astronomical events which present themselves as rather obvious possibilities. I shall explain them more fully in the next chapter. They are the Spring Equinox, the Summer Solstice, the Autumn Equinox and the Winter Solstice which are fairly readily observable turning points in the year of the seasons. For example, the Summer Solstice occurs on a day on which, for an observer north of the Tropic of Cancer, the Sun rises and sets furthest north of due east and west respectively and casts the shortest shadow at midday; the Winter Solstice occurs on a day when the Sun rises and sets furthest south and casts the longest shadow at midday; the equinoxes occur on days when the Sun rises and sets due east and west respectively and when the period between sunrise and sunset and the period between sunset and sunrise are equal. All these things are not easy to determine exactly within a day without moderately sophisticated observational aids (sighting devices, clocks of some sort and so on) but they can be approximated with quite primitive aids to about plus or minus a day if one knows what one is looking for and is not hampered by too many preconceptions. Meteorological variations can, of course, well confuse the matter, because, though in a rough way, major meteorological events are related to the four turning points in the year just discussed, they determine the seasons which are so important for agrarian peoples.

In choosing March at an early stage as the first month of the year, the Romans seem to have aiming at something a little before the Spring Equinox for the start of the year. When they switched to 1 January they were turning possibly to a few days after the Winter Solstice or even to the Winter Solstice. The Chinese favoured a month or so after the Winter Solstice in order to include what for them was the advent of Spring. The Babylonians stuck faithfully to the new Moon (for them a first visible crescent after sunset) on or about the Spring Equinox. This too seems to have been the early Jewish start of the year, though the Jews for religious purposes later shifted to the new Moon on or about the Autumn Equinox. Some Greek states favoured a new Moon on or about the Summer Solstice though most adopted a new Moon on or about one of the equinoxes. In England as in other parts of Western Europe, 25 December, erroneously taken to be the Winter Solstice in the Julian calendar, was favoured in medieval times; it was replaced towards the end of the middle ages by 25 March, erroneously taken to be the Spring Equinox. These two dates are a matter of some interest. Fairly early in the first millennium AD they came to be accepted as the anniversaries of Christ's birthday (Christmas) and conception (Annunciation or Lady Day) respectively. Christ's alleged birthday, 25 December, seems to have been borrowed from the Roman Sun-worshipping celebration *Dies Natalis Solis Invicti* or the Winter Solstice wrongly fixed in the third century AD. Christ's incarnation or conception was then fixed nine months earlier. Thus the anniversaries of the incarnation and birth of Christ were fixed days in the Julian calendar, equated to the traditionally accepted but not actual dates of the Spring Equinox and Winter Solstice in that calendar. In the same period, the dating of Easter, still tied roughly to the Jewish calendar, was a matter for hot dispute. The Jewish Passover was the day of the full Moon after the Spring Equinox within the context of a luni-solar calendar which I shall later explain. Jesus was held to have celebrated this feast on a Thursday evening (to use a planetary day name) with his apostles, to have been crucified on the following day, to have lain in the tomb on the Jewish Sabbath and to have risen on the next day, Sunday or the first day of the Jewish week. Easter was the anniversary of the resurrection but instead of locating it in the Julian calendar already in operation the early Christians located it, with some qualifications, in the Jewish luni-solar calendar. Easter, overlooking some of these qualifications, is the first Sunday on or after the first full Moon after the Spring Equinox. Many words, much ink, some excommunication and possibly some blood were expended over what was the proper interpretation of this rule. R. R. Newton (1972, ch. 2) gives a lucid account of the sources of the controversy over the dating of Easter.

After Diocletian's reconquest of Egypt in AD 297, a 15-year fiscal cycle, the Indiction, was introduced. It began on 1 September. This practice spread elsewhere in the Roman Empire and led to 1 September being regarded as the start of the year. This persisted in the Eastern Church long after the demise of the Western Roman Empire although it gave way after a much shorter time in the West to the other dates

9

already mentioned. In England, as already reported, for the greater part of the Middle Ages 25 December was favoured though it later gave way to 25 March (see Poole, 1969). Only in AD 1752 when the English Parliament belatedly adopted the Gregorian calendar reform was 1 January restored as the start of the year.

Some preliminary remarks on Gregory's revision of the Julian calendar will be appropriate at this point. Julius Caesar, recognizing that the official year was markedly out of phase with the seasons, set out to restore the seasons to more traditional Roman dates. He added 90 days to the year we now call 46 BC so that 1 January in the year we now call 45 BC occurred 7 days after the Winter Solstice and for 45 BC and later years added a day or two to several months to make the 12 of them total 365 days, the length of the long established Egyptian civil year. Previously they had totalled 355 days in years which did not have an intercalated month and 377 or 378 days in years which had the intercalary month. Julius decreed that in every fourth year February should have an extra or twentyninth day. Thus the average length of the year was set to 365.25 days. Ptolemy III Euergetes in 238 BC had tried unsuccessfully to add a three hundred and sixty-sixth day every fourth year to the standard 365-day Egyptian year in order to achieve a closer approximation to the solar tropical year. Sosigenes, Julius' adviser, may have been aware of this attempt and the astronomical argument for it. I should be quite surprised if he were unaware of Hipparchos' estimate of the year, made less than a century prior to the time he was helping Julius, namely 365.2467 days for the tropical year.

Sosigenes may have felt that a simple rule for adding a three hundred and sixty-sixth day to each fourth year was near enough. Taking Hipparchos' estimate to be correct, in some 303 years the calendar would be a day out of step with the seasons but that discrepancy should worry no one. In 606 years, it would be two days out but perhaps some later Pontifex Maximus would make some further correction. If Julius Caesar were willing to add 90 days to what we call 46 BC some later pontiff should be willing to subtract a day or two. All this, of course, is somewhat idle speculation. As it happens, even Hipparchos' estimate was slightly too great and in fact after 130 years the Julian calendar was a day out of step with the true tropical year. By AD 325, when some 200 to 300 bishops mainly from the East assembled in Nicaea under Constantine to try to settle the dating of Easter, the Arian heresy and some other contentious matters, they recognized that the Spring Equinox had moved forward to about 21 March. Being resolute, they thought they could settle this issue by declaring that in future 21 March would be the date of the Spring Equinox. However, it continued to move inexorably forward in the Julian calendar. By AD 1582, Pope Gregory, like Julius with good astronomical advice, found the Equinox to be occurring on or about 11 March. He took two radical decisions. First, he cancelled 10 calender days, declaring the day following 4 October, AD 1582 to be 15 October. Second, to minimize such future drastic action, he decreed that centurial years except those exactly divisible by 400 be ordinary years of 365 days. Thus AD 1600 and 2000 were to be leap years but AD 1700, 1800 and 1900 were to be ordinary years. In a span of four centuries the average length of the calendar year was by the latter rule to be 365.2425 days; it was still too long but it will not call for any further correction by more than a day for about three millennia.

The final information to be provided in this introductory chapter concerns the numbering of the years in the Christian Era, traditionally regarded as beginning from the birth or from the incarnation of Christ. Early opinion, as we have seen, set these events to the Winter Solstice and the Spring Equinox respectively in the year we would label today 1 BC, though for someone who regarded the year as beginning in September or on 25 December, the birth would be placed in AD 1. Some exegetical opinion places the events 2, 3 or 4 years earlier. The details of the argument involve the date of the end of Herod's reign and the date of Roman overlordship in Palestine but they are irrelevant to my present concern. Had the Romans required the registration of births within the territories under their control they would perhaps have recorded the year we call 1 BC as the twentysixth in Augustus' regnal period or they would have recorded it as the year in which Cossus Cornelius Lentulus and Lucius Calpurnius Piso were Consuls. The Jews number the years from the creation of the world, allegedly in what we call 3761 BC; the Mohammedans number them from the flight of the prophet from Mecca in AD 622. After the establishment of the Seleucid dynasty in Babylonia in the late fourth century BC the years were numbered there from the beginning of the dynasty. There are many different conventions concerning eras.

In that we now call AD 532 Dionysius Exiguus proposed as an alternative to other cycles of years for use in fixing Easter dates one of 532 years (see Fotheringham, 1931 and Poole, 1969). He regarded one such cycle as having just been completed, the one beginning in the alleged year of the incarnation of Christ, that is what we call 1 BC. Using the other rules involved in his system, he worked out Easter dates for the first few decades of the second cycle beginning in AD 532 and others later extended the calculations for further periods. In the West the system steadily won favour over others using other cycles, though there seems to have been no intention at first to use it for chronographic purposes. The dating of Easter was one of the many issues on which there were disputes in England which had been christianized from the north by the Celtic missionaries and from the south by the Roman missionaries. At the Synod of Whitby in AD 644, the various issues discussed there were settled in favour of Rome—the dating of Easter, the way to cut a tonsure, the recognition of the primacy of the Bishop of Rome as St Peter's successor and so on. The very learned Venerable Bede (*circa* 673–735) was familiar with all this and with the Dionysian cycle. Among his works is an essay on the calendar, *De Temporis*, in which he remarks that some periods are determined by nature (he instanced the year), some by tradition (he instanced the Julian months) and some by authority or arbitrary decision (e.g., the 7-day week). In his great *History of the Church in England*, looking for a way of specifying the years he resorted to the Dionysian years after the incarnation of Christ. Indeed, in his second chapter he reports that the preparations for the invasion by Julius Caesar of Britain were made in the six hundred and ninety-third year from the foundation of the city of Rome or the sixtieth year before the incarnation of our Lord. His convention was taken by the English missionaries into the Frankish Kingdom and later Charlemagne, establishing a new Roman Empire in Western Europe, made it official in the greater part of the West. It spread somewhat later to Eastern Christendom.

Thus our hours, minutes and seconds are the heritage from a first century BC Hellenistic astronomer based on some mixture of much earlier Egyptian and Babylonian arbitrary conventions. This same astronomer departed from these models in giving us midnight for the separation of the days. Our week has Jewish religious and Hellenistic astrological origins but both may be derived in part at least from Babylonia. Our months are derived from early Roman Imperial months which in turn are derived from Republican Roman practices: all the names are Roman and the number of days in each is Julian. Though we call them 'months' they are not in any strict sense Moon periods. Our ordinal numbering of the days in the months, however, is not Roman. The leap year rule is that of Julius Caesar modified by a Roman Pope in AD 1582, intended to yield on average a near solar tropical year. Our use of 1 January as the beginning of the year is Republican Roman in origin though for a long time it was not observed in England and was only restored to use in AD 1752. Our numbering of the years derives from the use by an early great English historian of a rule devised for another purpose, the troublesome matter of dating Easter.

What a strange hodge-podge in which nothing quite fits anything else! The weeks don't quite fit the months of the year; to make the months fit the year real Moon periods are abandoned; the years are never exact solar tropical periods though on average they are good approximations. We shall see later that the days are not quite what they are made out to be, for example, midday by the clock is usually not quite midday by the Sun though we think of the days as being determined by the cycle of appearances and disappearances of the Sun in the sky.

In the next chapter I shall discuss in greater detail those recurrent astronomical phenomena which have been used to greater or less extent by calendar makers, what Bede called periods determined by nature. In later chapters I shall discuss the traditions or conventions and the arbitrary decisions in calendars which are like or different from our own in various ways. These presentations of other traditions and decisions will involve a little preliminary repetition of much that has been set forth in this and the next chapter.

2/SOME BASIC ASTRONOMICAL EVENTS

The calendar-makers with whom I am concerned were guided by the rising of stars and other celestial bodies in the east and by their setting in the west, by the movement of the Sun, the Moon and five other wanderers among the so-called fixed stars, by the phases of the Moon and by the coming into conjunction with the Sun of various bright stars and of the other wanderers. Though the Babylonians charted these events and the Greeks developed theories to explain these phenomena, I shall account for them in modern terms and give recently established quantities when these are relevant. There are numerous introductory astronomical textbooks in which the reader may find a fuller or a more lucid exposition. Among the more formal but not unduly formal are Spencer Jones (1934), Payne-Gaposchkin (1961) and Wood (1967). An illuminating but more popularly oriented book is *The Flammarion Book of Astronomy* (1964). In this and some following chapters I shall occasionally refer to particular stars or constellations. The reader is urged to look up their locations in some star chart, for instance *Norton's A Star Atlas and Reference Book* (1957).

I shall discuss first the rotation of the Earth and then introduce the revolution of the Earth around the Sun. These will provide the data for the day and year. The next task will be to introduce the Moon's revolution in conjunction with the Earth around the Sun. This, added to the preceding material, will account for the lunar month. Finally, it will be necessary to introduce the revolution of Venus and of Jupiter around the Sun in order to account for the Venus and the Jupiter periods used by some calendar-makers.

The Earth rotates at a relatively constant rate around its axis, though the rate is slowly decreasing. For an observer at the terrestrial equator a star which is seen to rise due east early in the night will be seen to pass through the zenith and to set due west. For an observer north of the equator the same star will be seen to rise due east and to set due west but when it is at its highest point it will be south of the zenith by

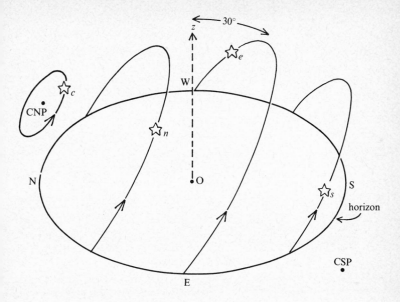

Fig. 2.1 The apparent paths of four stars for an observer, 0, at 30°N in terrestrial latitude. The zenith, *z*, is directly over his head. A star such as *e* which rises due east and sets due west traces the Celestial Equator which is tilted 30°S of the Zenith; its visible path is half a circle. Stars such as *n* and *s* also follow a path tilted south by 30°, *n* tracing more than half a circle and *s* less than half above the horizon. A star such as *c*, a circumpolar, never cuts the horizon; the centre of its circle is the Celestial North Pole, (CNP). Below the southern horizon is the Celestial South Pole, (CSP).

the same number of degrees as he is north of the equator. But wherever the observer is positioned on the Earth, the path of such a star traces for him the Celestial Equator lying in the plane perpendicular to the axis of the Earth's rotation. For an observer located appreciably north of the terrestrial equator, there are some stars which trace during the night arcs of circles which do not dip below the horizon. These are for him circumpolar stars; the further north he is the more of them there are. The centre of the concentric circles traced by these circumpolars is the Celestial North Pole to which the axis of the Earth points (see Fig. 2.1). At present the star Polaris or *alpha Ursae Minoris* is very near to this point. For an observer located appreciably south of the

15

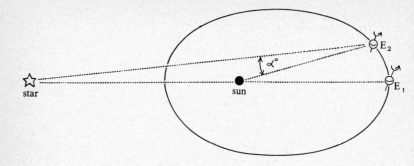

Fig 2.2   As the Earth rotates in approximately one day it revolves
around the Sun in approximately 365.25 days. Thus on occasion E_1, the
Sun and some fixed star will be in conjunction, whereas the occasion
E_2, the Sun and that fixed star will be separated by $\alpha°$. On average the
Earth's rotation requires about 4 minutes per day to cover this angle.

equator, the centre of the part circles described by the analogous
southern circumpolars is the Celestial South Pole.

A star crossing the meridian, the imaginary line running through
the zenith and between the celestial poles, is said to be in culmination.
Intervals between successive culminations of a star located on the
Celestial Equator are at present about 23 hours 56 minutes 4.1 seconds
as measured by the clock. This is the period of rotation of the Earth
and is also the sidereal day. In the remote past it was only very slightly
less.

While the Earth has been rotating once relative to the fixed stars,
it has been moving along its orbit of revolution around the Sun on
average almost 0.99° per day. Thus a small further fraction of rotation
will have to occur between successive meridian crossings by the Sun
because the Sun has moved eastward among the fixed stars (see Fig.
2.2). On average these periods are 24 hours as measured by the clock;
this is the mean solar day.

The plane of the Celestial Equator is tilted by about 23.5° to the
plane of the orbit of revolution of the Earth. This accounts, as we shall
see, for the Sun being north of the Celestial Equator in summer and
south in winter (see Fig. 2.3). The Sun's apparent path in the heavens
relative to the fixed stars is called the Ecliptic for a reason which will be
given later. The angle of about 23.5° between the Ecliptic and the
Celestial Equator is spoken of as the obliquity of the Ecliptic.

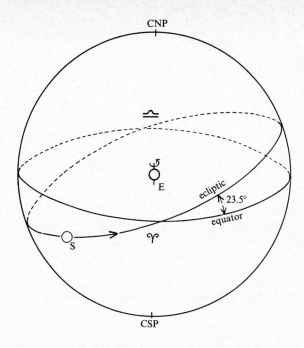

Fig 2.3   The Celestial Sphere is the apparent sphere as seen by an
observer on the Earth (E) on the inner surface of which the celestial
bodies, the fixed stars, the Sun, the Moon and the planets, seem to move.
In the case of the fixed stars, apart from proper motion detectable only
over substantial periods of time, the apparent motion is the result of the
rotation of the Earth. The North and South Celestial Poles (CNP and
CSP) are points in the Sphere fixed by the axis of the Earth's rotation.
These points change slowly in concert with the precession of the
equinoxes. The Celestial Equator is defined by the plane perpendicular
to the Earth's axis and is traced by any star which rises due east and
sets due west. The Sun moves west-to-east and north-to-south during a
tropical year amongst the fixed stars, tracing the Ecliptic which is offset
to the Celestial Equator by about 23.5°. The Sun is north of the Equator
during Summer and south during Winter in the northern hemisphere.

The orbit of the Earth's revolution around the Sun departs slightly
from a circle, being an ellipse with the Sun at one of its foci. The
deviation from strict circularity is spoken of as the eccentricity of the

17

Earth's orbit. As implied in Kepler's second law of planetary motion, the Earth has greater angular velocity when nearest the Sun (perihelion) than when furthest from it (aphelion).

Though the mean solar day is 24 hours, the actual intervals between successive solar meridian crossings varies around this value as anyone who has read the time from a sun-dial knows. Four times a year the Sun makes its meridian crossing at 12 noon by the clock (on or about 15 April, 15 June, 31 August and 24 December). There are four peaks of departure from 12 noon: the solar meridian crossing is at about 11.56 a.m. in mid-May, about 12.06 p.m. in late July, about 11.44 a.m. at the beginning of November and about 12.14 p.m. approaching mid-February. This difference between the mean solar day and the apparent solar day, called the equation of time, is the product of two main factors. First, the eccentricity of the Earth's orbit results in a slight apparent speeding up (between aphelion and perihelion) and a slight apparent slowing down (between perihelion and aphelion) of the Sun's progression through the fixed stars. This accounts for a difference of ± 7.5 minutes. Second, the obliquity of the Ecliptic adds an independent apparent variation of the Sun's pace measured between celestial meridians of Right Ascension perpendicular to the Equator. At the solstices the Sun is moving roughly parallel to the Equator, so 1° of motion on the Ecliptic is about 1° of motion relative to the Equator. At the equinoxes the Ecliptic is tilted 23.5° to the Equator. It may help the reader to think here of a right-handed triangle in which the hypotenuse meets the base at 23.5° Perpendiculars dropped from the hypotenuse at unit intervals will be separated by something less than one unit along the base. Were it not for the eccentricity of the Earth's orbit, the Sun would make its meridian crossings at 12 noon on the equinoxes and solstices, running behind or ahead by up to about 9.5 minutes between these events. The two effects when joined produce the variations expressed in the equation of time. For a fuller explanation see any standard text-book of astronomy such as Spencer Jones (1934).

Were calendar-makers to use the intervals between successive solar meridian crossings as the day, such days would vary one from another over a range of about 51 seconds, important for an astronomical calendar but insignificant in one for every-day practical use.

A further variation is introduced for those who measure the day from sunrise to sunrise or from sunset to sunset provided they are located appreciably north of the terrestrial equator. The variation increases with the observer's displacement from the terrestrial equator. For an observer at 30°N. the period between successive sunrises decreases by about 1 minute per day around the Spring Equinox and increases by about 1 minute around the Autumn Equinox; for an observer at 60°N., the period increases and decreases by about 3 minutes respectively on these occasions. These too are not variations likely to disturb the calendar-makers with whom I am concerned. For observers within the Arctic and Antarctic circles, the Sun does not rise or set for some days at the relevant Solstices. I shall not, however, be discussing any calendars made by inhabitants of these regions and so shall not discuss their problems.

When two celestial bodies, say the Sun and the Moon or the Sun and some fixed star, come level with each other in respect of their east-west apparent locations (there are two ways of assessing this, along the Celestial Equator or along the Ecliptic, which give slightly different results but at this point I shall ignore the difference), they are said to be in conjunction. When they are 180° apart they are said to be in opposition, for example one is setting when the other is rising. I shall leave for the moment conjunctions between the Sun and the Moon or between the Sun and other wanderers such as Venus and Jupiter. When a bright star on or near the Ecliptic, such as Regulus, *alpha Leonis*, is first seen rising just before sunrise (this is called its heliacal rising) it is just past conjunction with the Sun. When it is last seen setting just after sunset (its heliacal setting) it is approaching conjunction with the Sun. The interval between such conjunctions is some 365.25636042 days for the epoch AD 1900 and it is slowly increasing by 0.00000012 days per century. This is the period of the Earth's revolution around the Sun. It is also the sidereal year. It is, however, slightly longer than the year of the seasons which is more important for calendar-makers.

Not only does the Sun appear to move eastward among the fixed stars, completing a full circle in 365.25636042 days, but also, because of the obliquity of the Ecliptic to the Equator, it appears to move north and south of the Equator. It spends about 186 days 11 hours north of the Equator and about 178 days 19 hours south of it. In the former period the Earth turns more of its northern hemisphere to the Sun, so temperatures in that hemisphere are higher, the hours of daylight longer, the Sun is higher in the sky at midday and the Sun casts the shortest shadows at points above 23.5°N. In the latter period the reverse of each of these holds. In midsummer, the Sun reaches its most northerly apparent position. Up till then it has been moving steadily northward, then for a day or so it seems to stand still (relative to its north-south location). This is the Summer Solstice, a term derived from the Latin, *Sol stetit*, the Sun stood still. For an observer at 23.5°N., that is, on the tropic of Cancer, the Sun is at the zenith on this occasion. In midwinter, the Sun reaches its most southerly apparent position; this is the Winter Solstice. About midway through its northward journey between the Winter and Summer Solstices it crosses the Celestial Equator. On that occasion it rises and sets due east and west respectively and the periods of sunlight and of night (including the two twilights) are equal, hence the term 'equinox'. This is the Spring Equinox. Midway through its southward journey it crosses the Equator again. This is the Autumn Equinox.

The interval between successive Spring Equinoxes is a little less than the sidereal solar year (which is the period of the Earth's revolution around the Sun). This discrepancy results from gravitation and from the joint facts that the Earth has an equatorial bulge and that the Equator is oblique to the Ecliptic. Just as a spinning top has a wobble in its axis of rotation so does the Earth. The wobble in the Earth's case is slow, taking a period of 25,800 years (see Fig. 2.4). The axis of rotation points now in the north, as was said above, almost to the star Polaris, whereas some 12,900 years ago, that is about 10950 BC, it pointed, in terms of present orientation, some 47° south to a point in the constellation of *Hercules*. When the pyramid of Cheops was built about 2700 BC, the star Thuban, *alpha Draconis*, was the pole star. Every clear night in that epoch Thuban shone down a passage built into that pyramid parallel to the polar axis.

Another effect of this slow wobble of the axis of the Earth is a sliding backward along the Ecliptic of the points where the Celestial Equator cuts that circle. When the Babylonians first identified the twelve zodiacal constellations, on which they later based their twelve Signs of the Zodiac, the Sun crossed the Equator at springtime in the constellation named the Bull-of-Heaven. As the Babylonians regarded the year as beginning at the Spring Equinox, this constellation is said sometimes to have been called the Bull-in-front as well as the Bull-of-Heaven. Virgil wrote in *The Georgics*, though about two millennia out of date,

> The gleaming white bull with his golden horns
> opens the year.

In Virgil's time the spring crossing occurred in the zodiacal constella-

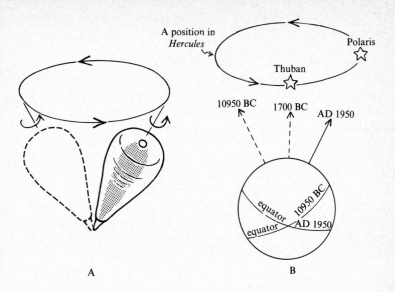

Fig 2.4   A. The wobble of a spinning top. B. The analogous wobble of the spinning Earth. The Celestial North Pole describes a circle subtending 47° in 25,800 years. In AD 1950 the Celestial North Pole almost coincided with the star Polaris, in 2700 BC it almost coincided with Thuban and in 10950 BC it was in the constellation *Hercules*. As a result of this slow wobble the points where the Equator cuts the Ecliptic slowly slide back along the latter—the precession of the equinoxes.

tion of the Ram. Now it occurs in the constellation of the Fishes and in the early third millennium AD it will occur in the constellation of the Watercarrier. Thus the spring equatorial crossing-point has been sliding backward along the Ecliptic. This phenomenon, called the precession of the equinoxes, is said to have been discovered by the Greek astronomer Hipparchos in about 130 BC (see Pannekoek, 1961, pp. 124–7). Claims have been made for an earlier discovery by Kidinnu in Babylon (but see Neugebauer, 1950).

The word Zodiac derives from the Greek *zoon*, an animal. It was called *kuklos zodiakus*, the animal circle (which I shall discuss at greater length in chapter 5). Most of the zodiacal constellations and signs had animal names: the ram, the bull, the crab, the lion, the scorpion, the fishes, the goat-horned one. Nevertheless, Chaucer's term 'The Circle of the Beasts' is a little hard on the twins, the virgin, the scales and the water-carrier, if not on the archer traditionally conceived as a bow-carrying centaur.

The Babylonians from about 400 BC distinguished the zodiacal constellations, distinctive patterns of stars, from the Signs of the Zodiac which are 30° segments of a band about 17° wide centered on the Ecliptic. Since Hipparchos we refer to the spring crossing of the Equator by the Sun as the First Point of Aries (the constellation in which it was located when he made his distinction between the sidereal and the tropical years). The First Point of Aries is moving backward, that is west, along the Ecliptic by about 1° in 71.62 years or about 1.396° per century. Hipparchos, comparing his observations of the position of Spica, *alpha Virginis*, relative to the First Point of Aries with those made by Timocharis some 135 years earlier and his observation of the Summer Solstice with that made by Aristarchos some 145 years earlier, concluded that the precession amounted to about 40 seconds of arc per annum (a good result as the modern estimate is 50.3 seconds of arc). He concluded that the length of the tropical year, measured between successive Spring Equinoxes, was 365.24667 days which is only about 6 minutes 16 seconds too long — a remarkable approximation. He also knew that the sidereal year, measured from one heliacal rising of some star near the Ecliptic, to the next, was a little over 365.25 days.

Whereas the sidereal year is very slowly increasing, the tropical year is slowly decreasing. The currently accepted value for the latter is $(365.24219879 - .00000614T)$ days, where T are centuries after AD 1900. Using this value, the tropical year was

365.24249965 days	*circa* 3000 BC
365.24241055 days	*circa* 1500 BC
365.24231545 days	*circa* AD 1
365.24222335 days	*circa* AD 1500

The value .00000614 days per century amounts to about 5.3 seconds per millennium which is scarcely worth allowing for in any subsequent calculations, though I shall allow for it.

It is difficult to know whether the estimates of the year made earlier than Hipparchos were referring to the sidereal or the tropical year. From quite early times, the beginning of the third millennium BC or even earlier, the Egyptians settled on 365 days for their civil calendar, but after a time they seem to have discovered that they had set it about a quarter-day too short. In about 380 BC Eudoxos, the Greek astro-nomer, reported that the Egyptians had found the year to be 365.25 days. In 500 BC Naburimannu of Babylonia gave 365.2609 and in about 383 BC Kidinnu gave 365.236 as the length of the year (see Fotheringham, 1930). As the last date is about that of the introduction of a regular 19-year cycle of intercalations of an extra month in the Babylonian luni-solar calendar, Kidinnu's estimate is probably of the tropical year. In which case, it is too short by .00633 days or about 9 minutes. Liu Hsin produced in China an estimate of 365.250162 days during the seventh century BC (see Needham, 1959). One of the most accurate pre-modern determinations was that of Omar Khayyam, the Persian astronomer, mathematician and poet, in AD 1079. His value was 365.24242 days, only .000166 days or only about 14 seconds too long at the time he made it.

As the Sun requires almost 365.25 days for its apparent eastward movement among the fixed stars from one Spring Equinox to the next, it progresses at an average rate of 0.9856° per day along the Ecliptic. Because of the eccentricity of the Earth's orbit, the apparent eastward movement, as we have seen, is not uniform. This may be shown by giving the number of days, to the nearest one-hundredth, which the Sun took in 1938 to move through each Sign of the Zodiac, each sign being a 30° segment as measured along the Ecliptic (data from *The Nautical Almanac for* 1938).

	Days			Days	
Aries	30.46	} spring 92.76	*Libra*	30.38	} autumn 89.84
Taurus	30.98		*Scorpio*	29.90	
Gemini	31.32		*Sagittarius*	29.56	
Cancer	31.48	} summer 93.66	*Capricornus*	29.40	} winter 88.98
Leo	31.28		*Aquarius*	29.60	
Virgo	30.90		*Pisces*	29.98	

The Earth and the Moon revolve around the Sun as a pair, revolving around each other as they do so. As the mass of the Earth is much greater than that of the Moon the centre of gravity of the pair is much closer to the Earth's centre than to the Moon's. Indeed the centre of gravity of the pair is inside the surface of the Earth. It is this centre of gravity which revolves around the Sun in a nearly true ellipse (it is, of course, perturbed a little by the varying gravitational pulls of Venus, Mars, Jupiter etc.). The Earth 'clumps' around this orbit like a wheel with an off centre hub. Though the Moon revolves around the Sun in a slightly wavy path, it is easy to think of the Moon as revolving around the Earth regarded as a fixed point. If at a given time on one evening the Moon is seen in conjunction with some fixed star it will be seen to be about 13° east of that star at the same time on the next evening, and on average back in conjunction with it after 27.32166 days. This is the sidereal lunar month which varies from about 27.03 days to about 27.61 days as a result of the eccentricity of the Moon's orbit around the Earth and of the eccentricity of the pair's orbit around the Sun. The Moon appears to be passing through the fixed stars more rapidly when it is nearest the Earth (at perigee) than when furthest (at apogee). For one year (which I checked in *The Nautical Almanac*) the Moon in one day moved 15° in longitude at perigee and 11° at apogee; these may not be extreme values.

Though the Moon makes a circuit of the stars in about 27.32 days, the Sun moves on from where it was at the beginning of this period by about 1° per day. Thus it takes the Moon a little more than two additional days on average to catch up with the Sun. The period between successive conjunctions of the Sun and the Moon averages at present 29.5305879 days or 29 days 12 hours 44 minutes 2.79 seconds. This is the synodic lunar month. It varies from about 29.26 days to about 29.80 days. It is also increasing very slowly by about .00000019 days or less than two hundredths of a second per century (value given in *The Indian Ephemeris and Nautical Almanac for the year* 1967). In later calculations I shall ignore this very slight increase.

We see the Moon, not because of its own light as in the case of the Sun and the fixed stars but mainly because of the light falling on it from the Sun which it reflects. Just as sunlight reflected by the Moon illuminates the Earth on a moonlit night, so sunlight reflected by the Earth illuminates the Moon; so on suitable occasions we can see in the earth-shine part of the Moon which is not illuminated by the Sun— the old Moon in the arms of the new is the poetic description. When the Moon is in conjunction with the Sun, its Sun-illuminated side faces away from us; so we cannot see it. When it is in opposition, its Sun-illuminated side faces us; so we see it as a full Moon. In between we see it as a crescent Moon, a half Moon and a gibbous Moon. Thus a day or two after conjunction we see it as a thin crescent in the Western sky just after sunset. When it was important for calendar-makers, the new crescent was sometimes called 'the knife of time'. It is often called a 'New Moon' but that phrase is used by astronomers for the conjunction. On the next evening after its first visibility, the crescent Moon is a bit fatter and about 13° higher above the horizon. About 7 days after

24

conjunction we see it near the meridian as a half Moon just after sunset. About 14 or sometimes 15 days after conjunction we see it rising in the east as a full Moon just about sunset. Thereafter, it rises later and later after sunset reducing in shape from full through gibbous and half to crescent. Strictly speaking 'crescent' should be applied only to the initial sickle shape as the word originally meant 'growing', but it would be pedantic not to describe the thin sickle seen rising just before sunrise as crescent. These shape changes constitute the phases of the Moon and occupy, as we have seen, on average 29.5305879 days.

It is customary to speak of four quarters of the Moon. The first is from conjunction or New Moon to the First Quarter (when the waxing Moon appears a half-disc), from the First Quarter to the Full Moon, from the Full Moon to the Last Quarter (when the waning Moon becomes a half-disc again) and from the Last Quarter to the next New Moon. In Table 2.1 are set out the lengths in days, hours and minutes of the four quarters of six successive lunar months, the first beginning at 15 hours 42 minutes after midnight, 4 January 1973. It will be noticed that in rounded days, the quarter lasts about 7 or 8 days, the 7-day periods being rather more frequent than the 8-day periods.

Some very accurate early estimates of the lunar synodic periods were made. In Babylonia, in about the early seventh century BC, the

	(i) conjunction and first quarter			(ii) first quarter and full Moon			(iii) full Moon and last quarter			(iv) last quarter and next conjunction		
	d.	h.	m.	d.	h.	m.	d.	h.	m.	d.	h.	m.
1.	7	13	55	6	16	1	7	8	27	7	3	18
2.	7	4	42	6	20	2	7	17	3	7	20	57
3.	6	21	19	7	2	7	7	23	7	7	12	5
4.	6	16	42	7	9	18	8	4	8	7	2	56
5.	6	15	12	7	16	51	8	3	42	6	19	54
6.	6	19	39	7	20	24	7	23	8	6	15	56

Intervals between

Table 2.1 Duration in days, hours and minutes of the four quarters of the first 6 lunar synodic months of 1973, the first conjunction being at 15 hours and 42 minutes after midnight on 4 January. Notice that fourteen quarters are 7 days to the nearest rounded day and ten are 8 days. (Based on data in *The Nautical Almanac for the Year* 1973)

average lunation was taken to be about 29.53139 days. In about 500 BC according to Fotheringham (1930) Naburimannu found it to be 29.530614 days and in perhaps 383 BC Kidinnu found it to be 29.530594 days, a period which was used when the 19-year cycle of 235 lunations (the Metonic cycle) was introduced in 383 BC or in 367 BC in Babylonia and which is used in the modern Jewish calendar. The Chinese oracle-bones, *circa* thirteenth century BC, imply a synodic lunar month of 29.53 days. In the third century AD Yang Wei gave a value of 29.530598 days (Needham, 1959). In about AD 682 the Mayans in Central America equated 149 lunations with 4,400 days which yields an average lunar month of 29.5302 days. In about AD 1000 the Mayans equated 405 lunations with 11,960 days which yields an average lunar month of 29.530864 days. Neither of these is as close as Naburimannu's or Kidinnu's or Yang's estimates but they are amazing nevertheless.

The plane of the Moon's orbit of revolution around the Earth is tilted by about $5°8'$ to the plane of the Earth's orbit around the Sun (describing the Ecliptic). Thus on most of the occasions when the Sun and the Moon are in conjunction or in opposition the Moon is north or south of the Ecliptic. When the Moon is on or very near the Ecliptic at conjunction there is an eclipse of the Sun and on or very near it at opposition an eclipse of the Moon. Hence the term Ecliptic for which I promised to account.

It is important to explain the interval which occurs between the lunar conjunction and the first visible crescent Moon. On rare occasions the first visible crescent occurs after sunset on the day (midnight to midnight) on which the conjunction has occurred quite early. More often it is on the next day or two. Two major factors involved are that (i) the Moon must be separated by about $7°$ from the Sun for its Sun-illuminated surface to be visible from the Earth (this is a consequence of the rugged mountainous surface of the Moon) and (ii) the Moon must be moderately high above the western horizon at sunset (otherwise it will set before the Sun is sufficiently below the horizon for the Sun's scattered light not to blot out the Moon's fainter reflected light). The interval of time for the Moon to become separated by $7°$ from the Sun depends upon (i) its separation at the time of conjunction (it may be up to $5°8'$ N. or up to $5°8'$ S. of the Ecliptic at the time of conjunction) and (ii) its apparent velocity at this time (as stated above, greatest at perigee and least at apogee). The height of the young Moon above the western horizon depends upon the angle of its apparent path to the horizon. This is steepest for an observer in the northern hemisphere when the Moon is most north of the Ecliptic at the Spring Equinox and shallowest when it is most south of the Ecliptic at the Autumn Equinox. Both angles become shallower the more north the observer is from the terrestrial equator. Both Parker (1950) and Neugebauer (1969) give lucid explications of all this. Schoch (1928) calculated that at the latitude of Babylon, 32°30′N., the minimum interval between conjunction and the first visible crescent is 16.5 hours and the maximum about 42 hours. The first crescent will not be visible in Babylon even on favourable occasions (Moon about 5°N. of the Ecliptic, the date near the Spring Equinox and the Moon near perigee) in the minimum period unless conjunction occurs about 16 hours before sunset, that is shortly after midnight. Schoch also states that the minimum and maximum periods for an observer at 51°N. (just south of London) are 20 hours and 63 hours respectively. Bickerman (1968) by contrast claims 23 hours and 69 hours respectively for an observer at Athens, 38°N., based apparently on observations rather than calculations and hence affected by viewing conditions. Bickerman, nevertheless, accepts Schoch's values for Babylon. For an observer at Athens he cites Ginzel's *Handbuch der Chronologie* (1906–14), a work I have not been able to consult. I find the values for Athens given by Bickerman incredible. Ashbrook (1971, 1972) cites modern observers in the high 40s and low 50s of latitude, admittedly knowing where to look and often using binoculars, seeing a first visible crescent only 18 or so hours after conjunction when the latter occurred shortly after midnight at about the time of the Spring Equinox (no doubt with the Moon near perigee and preferably north of the Ecliptic). I conclude from all this, that the first visible crescent occurs rarely on the day (reckoned from midnight) of conjunction, and more commonly on the first or second day after (and sometimes the third day after) depending on the time of the year and the latitude of the observer.

The other planets, which were known in antiquity, also never stray far north or south of the Ecliptic though none follows it exactly. The greatest departure is about 8.5° which defines the 17° width of the Zodiac.

The three planets whose orbits around the Sun are outside the Earth's, namely Mars, Jupiter and Saturn, periodically come into conjunction and opposition with the Sun. For most of the time they appear to be moving eastward among the stars like the Moon and the Sun but at an even slower rate than that of the Sun; that is, they are falling behind the Sun, on their eastward journey among the fixed stars,

27

Mars least rapidly and Saturn most rapidly. Thus the Sun catches up with Saturn after a shorter interval than that with which it catches up Mars. As these planets are approaching opposition they appear to be moving westward because the Earth on its smaller orbit is overtaking them. Just as trees in the foreground seen from a moving train seem to be moving backwards against the backdrop of more distant hills so these outer planets seem to be moving backward (or retrograde) against the background of the distant stars as the Earth begins to overtake them. In the middle of their retrograde phase of apparent motion they come into opposition with the Sun. As Venus and Mercury have orbits within that of the Earth, they are never in opposition to the Sun but they come into two conjunctions, one conjunction occurs when they are beyond the Sun relative to the Earth, the superior conjunction, and the other when they are between the Sun and the Earth, the inferior conjunction. At inferior conjunction they are in the midst of their retrograde (westward) apparent motion and appear to be falling behind the Sun; after that retrograde phase when they switch back into their direct (eastward) apparent motion, they appear to be overtaking the Sun or running ahead of it.

The sidereal and synodic periods of these planets (the former is the interval between successive conjunctions with some fixed star and is also the period of their revolution around the Sun and the latter is the interval between superior Solar conjunctions of Mercury and Venus or between Solar conjunctions of the other three) are as follows:

	Sidereal period	Synodic period
Mercury	88 days	116 days
Venus	225 days	584 days
Mars	687 days	780 days
Jupiter	11.9 years	399 days
Saturn	29.5 years	378 days

The Maya in Central America used the synodic period of Venus and the Hindus and the Chinese used Jupiter's sidereal period to generate periods longer than the solar year.

Though there is no shortage of readily observable astronomical periods for calendar-makers to use, most of them are variable by significant amounts or are difficult to distinguish. The tropical year which is relatively constant is difficult to distinguish from the sidereal year. The lunar synodic month is variable. Worst of all, these observable periods are not neat fractions or multiples of one another. How much easier it would have been if the month had 28 days, with the two half Moons and full Moon at the seventh, fourteenth and twenty-first days; if the tropical year were just 12 such months or 336 days; and if Jupiter's sidereal period were exactly 12 such years. But none of it comes out as neatly as this. The several periods almost fit but not quite; they are rather like the pieces of timber sawn up by the home carpenter. Added to these difficulties are the assorted conventions for taking fractions or multiples of some period such as the day, for example the seconds, minutes, hours and weeks. No wonder the writers of same of the apocrypha and of one of the Dead Sea Scrolls said in effect:

> Let us ignore the phases of the Moon, let us say the year is 364 days made up of four seasons of 91 days each and of 52 weeks of seven days on the seventh of which God bids us to rest. The fact that the ears are late in forming on the corn, that the fruit is late in ripening, that the solstices and equinoxes are delayed shows that God is punishing us for the sins of our neighbours (Beckwith, 1970).

3/THE DAY AND THE WEEK

Taking the day as some combination of daylight and night, there is, as we have seen in Chapter 1, some flexibility in determining just how it is to be defined or marked off. Setting it to the period from one sunrise (or one dawn) to the next, or to the period from one solar meridian crossing to the next or to the period from one sunset to the next results in a slightly more variable day than setting it to the period from one midnight to the next as measured by some uniformly running clock. Though the Egyptian practice of using the risings or settings of a succession of stars about 10° in longitude apart constituted a deficient 'clock', one which ran fast and then jumped backward, it has been the custom in the last century or two to check mechanical and electrical clocks against stellar meridian crossings. This assumes that the period of the Earth's rotation is constant. In addition to the fact that this period is slowly decreasing, it varies slightly from time to time. Hence, present day astronomers resort to an 'atomic clock' recording the more uniform oscillations in the internal structure of the atoms of certain elements. But this refinement need not worry us. For the purposes of this story a good mechanical chronometer, possibly even a good water-clock, is good enough.

Some years ago I visited a mosque in Istanbul about midday. I noticed an almanac hanging on the wall near the foot of the stairs leading to the top of the minaret. Apart from unfamiliar words it looked rather like the almanac I sometimes receive from the local grocer. As far as I can remember the months were Julian not Mohammedan, though at the time I was not well acquainted with the difference. The month was set out in weeks with the ordinal number of the day printed boldly in the centre of the relevant square. In the corner of each square was printed a smaller numeral in different colour. I asked my guide what the latter was. He told me it was the difference between watchtime and sundial time. He added that it was the duty of the muezzin to call the faithful to prayer when the Sun was half-way across the sky (that is, when it was making its meridian crossing). The inferior numeral was thus the correction in whole minutes required to bring mean solar time (clock time) to apparent solar time in accordance with the equation of time. As I listened to the beginnings of calls from various parts of the city spread over several minutes, it was clear that the callers had not co-ordinated their watches.

Quite early, ancient peoples divided the period of daylight into such obvious periods as dawn (from the disappearance of the stars until sunrise), morning (from sunrise until some time when the Sun is well up in the sky), the middle part of the day, the 'afternoon' in a more restricted sense ending at sunset, and evening or twilight (from sunset until the appearance of the stars). By means of some sort of sundial the period from sunrise to sunset could be subdivided more finely. The night, before the invention of clocks, could be divided by the position of recognizable stars in the sky, provided some scheme of successively replaceable marker stars had been developed.

Very early the Egyptians divided the period between sunrise and sunset into ten units, marked off by means perhaps of some sighting device such as a sundial, added two periods of twilight (early morning and evening) and divided the night into twelfths by means of star positions in the sky as already explained. Later, perhaps when they developed the water-clock, they divided both the daylight period, I presume including the two twilight periods and the night into twelfths. We have a surviving Egyptian water-clock, from the late second millennium BC and I assume that there were earlier examples which have not survived. The survivor is an ingenuous device. It was filled with water to the brim at the end of twilight. When the water had leaked out slowly through a hole in the bottom to bring the water level to a top marker inside the bowl the first hour had been completed. There were 3 columns of 12 markers, those for some seasons being more widely spaced than those for other seasons to allow for the different lengths of the night at different seasons of the year (see Parker, 1950, p. 40, also Neugebauer and Parker, 1960, pp. 116–21).

As pointed out earlier the twelve daylight Egyptian 'hours' were longest in summer (about 75 minutes), and shortest in winter (about 55.5 minutes) and the twelve night 'hours' were shortest in summer (about 45 minutes) and longest in winter (about 69.5 minutes). At the equinoxes the disparity was least, though if I am right in assuming that the Egyptians regarded morning and evening twilight as belonging to daylight, the hours of day and of night were never equal.

In Babylonia from an early stage the day, measured from sunset to sunset, was divided into twelve equal periods, each called a *beru*, presumably measured by some kind of clock. The *beru* was subdivided into thirty units, each called a *ges*, and each *ges* was subdivided into a sexagesimal fraction, a *gar*. Thus the *beru* was equal to about 2 hours in our terms, the *ges* to about 4 minutes and the *gar* to about 4 seconds. Later these units were also used for the measurement of something like what we now call the hour angles of stars and were subsequently adopted for all angular measurements. In the last usage the *ges* is 2° of angle and the *gar* is 2′ of angle. Our division of the circle into 360° is of Babylonian origin. An alternative Babylonian, and perhaps later, time system, divided daylight and night each into three watches each of which were divided into four 'temporal hours' analogous to the Egyptian 'temporal hours'. If I am right in assuming that the Babylonians regarded night as spanning from sunset to sunrise and daylight (strictly sunlight) from sunrise to sunset, then these 'temporal hours' would have been uniform at the equinoxes and would have later provided Hipparchos with his model for standard or uniform hours based on the equinoctial 'temporal hours'.

The Babylonian Kidinnu, it has been claimed, in the early fourth century BC produced astronomical tables using six uniform watches from midnight to midnight. He is said to have divided a watch into sixtieths, each called a *ges* equal to 4 minutes in our terms. He divided the *ges* into sixtieths, each a *gar*, equal to 4 seconds and further divided the *gar* into sixtieths, each equal to about .067 seconds, an interval of time which any clock available to him would not have been able to measure. Hipparchos subsequently substituted the division of the day from midnight to midnight into 24 standard or equinoctial hours and then followed the alleged Kidinnu scheme in successive subdivisions of sixtieths, that is, to use the later Latin terminology, the fractions were *pars minuta*, *pars secunda*, *pars tertia*, etc.

For astronomical purposes in the West and near East Hipparchos' standard hours measured from midnight or, after Ptolemy *circa* AD 150, from midday, prevailed but either 'temporal hours' or sun-dial hours were widely used for civil purposes. The deathknell of non-standard hours was struck in the West by the public clocks which tolled the hours from the fourteenth century onwards. It was too difficult to build a mechanical clock to strike 'temporal hours' or even hours related to the solar meridian crossings. Though these clocks were not perfect they struck something like Hipparchos' standard hours. Hence expressions such as '10 o'clock'. Though some 24-hour clocks were developed in Italy, most clocks in this period ran a 12 standard hour cycle set from mean midnight to mean midday in the first cycle and mean midday to mean midnight in the second.

Thus our hours, minutes and seconds measured from a clock-time midnight have their immediate remote origin in a Helenistic Greek convention, derived with some modification from an earlier Babylonian convention and in the case of the hours an even earlier Egyptian convention.

Like the Babylonian twelve *beru* units are the twelve *shih* periods into which the Chinese from early times divided the day. The latter were uniform units (hence equal to two equinoctial or standard hours). They were either counted from midnight or the first was centred on midnight. The *shih* was divided into eighths, or, in our terms, periods of 15 minutes. This use of twelfths and eighths by the Chinese is puzzling as their number system was decimal. However, as we shall see later they also used a complex set of sexagenary cycles. Possibly many of these things were borrowings from Babylonia, though the evidence of borrowing appears uncertain.

The Hindus, apparently after the Alexandrian conquests in the late fourth century BC and the subsequent setting up of the Greek kingdom in Bactria but possibly through direct contact with Hellenistic Greece, assimilated a great deal of Babylonian astronomical lore. They divided the day, beginning at sunrise, into sixty units, each a *ghati* (24 minutes in our terms), the *ghati* into sixty *palas* (24 seconds), the *pala* into sixty *vipalas* (0.4 seconds) and the *vipala* into sixty *vipratipalas* (about 0.0067 seconds, a period much too short for them to measure but no doubt useful in expressing the result of calculations). They were clearly in the grip of the Babylonian sexagesimal number system. When I come to discuss the Mayan calendrical systems I shall need to point to another people in an even firmer grip of a number system. The Sanskrit words *ghata*, *ghati* and *ghatika* mean a pot or by extension a water-clock (see MacDonell's *A Practical Sanskrit Dictionary*).

I shall now turn from the day to the week, the origin of which is more difficult to trace because it is even more a matter of convention. The year of the seasons of a little less than 365.25 days, but difficult of precise determination by early peoples, is important for an agrarian community. It is marked by the cycle of long-hot and short-cold periods of daylight, by the dropping of lambs, by the ripening of the corn, by the vintaging of grapes and many other important events. The month marked by the phases of the Moon is much easier to deter-

33

mine and is fairly easy to subdivide into rough quarters by means of the phases of the Moon, that is, (i) about midway in the invisibility between the last visible crescent before sunrise and the first visible crescent after sunset; (ii) the half waxing Moon; (iii) the full Moon and (iv) the half waning Moon, separated on average by about 7 or 8 days (see Chapter 2).

A month of 29 or 30 days is rather long for man to engage in continuous daily labour uninterrupted by a day off to visit the market to sell and buy wares, to transact other business and to hear the latest news and gossip. Even Jehovah, who may have been made in man's likeness, felt the need to rest on the seventh day after 6 busy days of creation. Had he reflected on what he had done he would have found it a day of anxiety rather than relaxation and would have recognized that it was his first and last day off if he were to keep the whole thing working thereafter. The stars did not keep pace with the Sun or the Moon with the Sun, large creatures had smaller ones to bite them and *vice versa*, and Adam, Eve, the serpent and the apple were in conjunction. No wonder he was on the point of washing it all out later.

The Meso-Americans seem to have something like a 5-day 'week', perhaps not because they were lazy but because one of their 'year' periods was 365 days which is neatly divisible into 5-day units. Some African peoples had a 4-day 'week'. The Romans had the *nundinum*, an 8-day period, the eighth day, the *nundinae* being a market day. The Egyptians divided their months of 30 days into three units of 10 days, a decade, during each of which a given star, called by the Greeks a decans, was the hour marker. I do not know, however, whether the tenth day was a market day or day of rest from ordinary labour. Webster (1916) is a mine of information on these short periods.

Our 7-day week emerged in two forms, the Jewish religious cycle of 7 days ending with the Sabbath or day of rest and religious observance and the planetary week of astrological significance in which each day bore the name of one of the seven planets known in antiquity, namely the Sun, Moon, Mars, Mercury, Jupiter (Jove), Venus and Saturn (see Colson, 1926). The word planet comes from the Greek *planetes*, the wanderers; these seven celestial bodies moved among the fixed stars. The Babylonians had a more picturesque name *bibbu*, the wild sheep, as these bodies broke through the fixed formation in which the tame sheep crossed the sky.

The Jewish day names are, in translation, First Day (our Sunday), Second Day, Third Day, ..., Sixth Day and Sabbath *(Shabbat)*.

If the Jewish week and planetary week did not have a common origin, they became assimilated at about the beginning of the Christian era. I suspect, however, that they both had their origin in Babylonian conventions.

The Jews in the Old Testament put great stress on keeping holy the Sabbath Day. We find Moses, in the pre-Babylonian exilic period, doing so. The parts of the Old Testament dealing with pre-exilic events may, however, well have been written or at least re-edited after the Exile in Babylon. Three derivations of the Hebrew word *Shabbat* have been suggested. First, it may be a variant of the Hebrew word for seven; thus 'the First Day' 'the Second Day' and so on but 'the Seventh' used as a noun. Second, it may be derived from the Hebrew verb 'to rest': the verb, of course, could have been derived from the noun, just as in English the verb 'to ski' comes from the noun 'ski'. Third, Langdon (1935) argues that it derives from the Akkadian word *sabbatu* or *sappatu* meaning 'the full Moon', which occurs on the fourteenth, the fifteenth (most usually) or the sixteenth day after conjunction or a day or two less after the first visible crescent.

Much earlier than the Jewish exile in Babylon, the Babylonians designated certain days in the lunar month as ones on which certain activities were proscribed. An Assyrian record dating from early in the first millennium BC and claiming an earlier derivation from Babylon (see Langdon, 1935), states that the physician should not heal, the seer prophesy, any man go out in the street or do anything desirable on the first, the seventh, the fourteenth, the nineteenth, the twenty-first, the twenty-eighth, the twenty-ninth (and if it occurred, the thirtieth) day of the month. The nineteenth day of the month was a sort of *dies irae* dedicated to an offended goddess. The other days correspond approximately to the first visible crescent Moon, the day of the waxing half Moon, the day of the full Moon, the day of the waning half Moon, the day of the last visible crescent and the day or days of the invisibility of the Moon. By the seventh century BC these days of regularly proscribed activities were reduced to the seventh, the fourteenth, (the nineteenth, the *dies irae*), the twenty-first and the twenty-eighth days of the month. We have here in effect the 7-day week with proscribed activities every seventh Sabbatarian day, geared approximately to the phases of the Moon, but, unlike both the Jewish week and the astrological planetary week, with a break of a day or two after a cycle of 4 'weeks'.

The Jews picked up their later month names in Babylonia without seeming to have appreciated the meanings of these Akkadian words translating Sumerian notions. Langdon could well be right in maintaining that they also picked up the 7-day cycle (making it continuous) and misapplied the Akkadian word *sabbatu* or *sappatu*.

The clearest early evidence on the planetary week, according to Colson (1926), is to be found in Roman writers in the first century BC identifying the Jewish *Shabbat* with Saturn's day together with more than a hint that they thought the Jews to be Saturn-worshippers. He cites clearer evidence from graffiti on the walls of Pompeii (hence earlier than AD 79 when Pompeii was overwhelmed by the eruption of Vesuvius). Some persons had scrawled on public walls, the planetary day names in Latin and in Greek, *Dies Solis*, *Dies Lunae*, *Dies Martis*, *Dies Mercurii*, *Dies Iouis*, *Dies Veneris* and *Dies Saturni*, and the *Theon hemerai* (days of the Gods), *Heliu*, *Selenes*, *Areos*, *Hermu*, *Dios*, *Aphrodites* and *Khronu*. Actually, whoever wrote the Latin graffito was only a tyro for he left out *Dies Mercurii*. The omission from the Latin list is included, however, in the parallel Greek list. I regard it as significant that the Greek example occurred. It may be merely that there were in Pompeii Romans literate in Greek but I suspect that it indicates that the planetary names were in use also among the Greeks at least in southern Italy.

Before I proceed with a discussion of other ancient evidence I should like to remark on three points. First, those in the realm of the Western Christian Church generally adopted the planetary day names, the Teutonic languages tending to substitute Twia for the Roman Mars, the dour Woden for the ebullient Roman Mercury, Thor for Jupiter (both hurlers of thunderbolts) and Fria or Frigga for Venus (both lusty goddesses). Those in the realm of the Eastern Church tended to adopt the Jewish practice, with one variation, Lord's Day, e.g., Modern Greek *Kyriaki* for the Jewish First Day, but then the Second Day, the Third Day and so on but *Sabbaton* or some variant of *Shabbat*, which also often worked its way into the Western nomenclature (see Appendix on p. 128). Second, the Mohammedan week-day names derive from the Jewish with 'Together' or 'Assembly' substituted for 'the Sixth Day', Friday being a day on which prayers were said in unison, whereas the Indian day names derive from the planetary week, presumably from a Hellenistic source. Third, whereas the Western planetary week and the Eastern Christian practice designated Sunday or the Lord's day, which followed the Jewish *Shabbat* or Saturn's day, as the first day of the week, naming of the days in the Slavic community clearly makes our Monday or their 'day after no activity' the first day of the week. As we shall see, on the best explanation of the order of the planetary day names, Saturday should be the first day of the week.

The seven 'planets' known in antiquity may be placed in order: (i) in terms of their maximum brightness; or (ii) in order of their sidereal periods; or (iii) in order of their synodic periods with the Sun. These orderings are not exhaustive but they are the most obvious for calendar-makers. In terms of decreasing brightness, the order is Sun, Moon, Venus, Jupiter, Mars, Saturn and Mercury. In terms of decreasing sidereal periods, it is Saturn, Jupiter, Mars, the Sun, Venus, Mercury and the Moon. In terms of synodic periods it is Mars, Venus, Jupiter, Saturn, (the Sun), Mercury and the Moon. None of these orders corresponds with the order of the names in the planetary week.

Dio Cassius, who wrote in the early third century AD, provided an ingenious explanation in astrological terms of the order of the planetary day names. Incidentally he said that in his time the convention was in widespread use (I suggest that we accept his testimony on this point), that it was of recent adoption (I have already cited evidence that it had been in use for about two centuries which seems to me scarcely to be recent) and that it was of Egyptian origin (if it were not Hellenistic as Neugebauer (1969) suggests, I suggest that it was Babylonian even though it may have come to Greece through Egypt).

Dio Cassius' explanation of the order of the planetary week-day names includes an astrological assumption that each planet is in successive control of an hour of the day and of being the regent of the day whose first hour it controls. Taking the planets in order of their sidereal periods, it is Saturn, Jupiter, Mars, the Sun, Venus, Mercury and the Moon. In terms of synodic periods it is Mars, Venus, Jupiter, Saturn, (the Sun), Mercury and the Moon. None of these orders seventh hours respectively of Saturn's day. Saturn succeeds to the role of controller in the eighth hour, the fifteenth hour and the twenty-second hour of his day. The twenty-third hour has Jupiter as controller and the twenty-fourth has Mars. The next hour, the first hour of the next day, has the Sun as controller so that day is the Sun's. The first hour, by subsequent successive replacement, of the third day has the Moon in control and so that day is the Moon's day. In like manner, Mars' day, Mercury's day, Jupiter's day and Venus' day follow.

If Dio Cassius' explanation of the order of the day names in the planetary week is historically correct, the inventors of the sequence must have had a twenty-four (not necessarily uniform) hour day. The sequence cannot be generated from the earlier Babylonian division of the day into twelve *berus*. At the time when the planetary week was emerging the Babylonians, the Egyptians, the Greeks (the astronomers at least) and the Romans were using a twenty-four-hour day.

According to Colson the planetary week spread over the Western Empire, rapidly and as a popular rather than official convention as part of the spread of astrology. Astrology was widely used in Babylonia but primarily in relation to the fortunes of the king and of the community as a whole. The casting of horoscopes for private persons seems to have been only a late Babylonian practice (see Sachs, 1952a). Possibly horoscopic astrology may have begun in Egypt or in Hellenistic Greece, in the latter of which the private person counted more. The Romans had always been a superstitious people, indeed the Latin word *religio* had more to do with magic, with scrupulous observance of rules warding off ill-luck than our word 'religion' connotes. The Romans like the Babylonians paid attention to auguries provided by the flight of birds, and by the state of the internal organs of sacrificial animals, the latter observations being a sort of early veterinary clinical pathology. They communicated much of this superstition to their conquered peoples and it was among the latter that both astrology and Christianity had strong appeals. Indeed by the early fourth century, despite the earlier protests of some of the Christian Fathers, the planetary week was regarded as a Christian convention.

Granted the identity of the Jewish Sabbath and Saturn's day, there was good reason for the early Christians to celebrate the Eucharist on the Sun's day or the Jewish First Day. Christ had observed the Passover with his chosen twelve on the day of the full Moon in the month beginning at or about the Spring Equinox. This was the Jewish Sixth Day, beginning at sunset on what we call Thursday. He said of the bread 'This is my body' and of the wine 'This is my blood' and sharing the bread and wine with them added 'Do this in remembrance of me'. Later on that day (sunset to sunset) he was betrayed, tried, crucified and laid in the tomb where his body rested during the Sabbath. On the Jewish First Day, possibly after midnight, that is on our Sunday, he rose from the dead. This miracle gave the First Day or Sunday a special significance and many early Christians adopted it as the day on which to commemorate him through the Eucharistic ceremony.

When the Emperor Constantine in about AD 321 officially adopted the planetary week he made out that he was doing so on Christian considerations. He had, it seems, been flirting for a long time with both Christianity and a Sun-worshipping cult perhaps related to Mithraism derived from Persia. When earlier he had seen, or dreamed, the Cross on the Sun's disc and.when on this occasion he officially adopted as Christ's special day what was also the Sun's day, he may have been hedging his bets (see Jones, 1949).

It is worth remarking that though Dio Cassius' astrological explanation of the order of planet names in the planetary week indicates that Saturday should be the first day, the Jewish custom of regarding the day after their Sabbath as the first day prevailed in the realms of the Western and Eastern Churches except in Slavic lands where the day 'after no activity' (that is Monday) was regarded as the first day. The Jewish convention flowed on directly to the Mohammedans and the week went indirectly through the Greeks (with the planetary names) to the Hindus.

The day as conceived above is determined by the apparent motion of the Sun, though in reality by the rotation of the Earth. We shall encounter a curious 'lunar day', the *tithi*, in Hindu calendrical practice, though there is good reason for believing that it was Babylonian in origin (Sachs, 1952 and Neugebauer, 1969). The lunar synodic month averaging a little over 29.53 days is divided into thirtieths each marked off by an increase of 12° in the separation of the Sun and the Moon. The first *tithi* begins at conjunction and ends when the Moon is 12° in longitude ahead of the Sun. The second *tithi* ends when the separation is 24° and so on. Though the average length of the *tithi* is about 23 hours 37 minutes it may be as short as about 21 hours or as long as about 26 hours as a result of the joint effect of the variable apparent angular velocities of the Sun and the Moon.

4/THE MONTH AND THE YEAR

The day which is the basic unit in every calendar is, as we have seen, definable in several ways, each yielding slightly different lengths of time. These differences, however, do not create serious problems for a calendar-maker. The serious problems arise in trying to reconcile the periods of the Moon and of the Sun expressed in whole days. There is a nest of problems here. First, any attempt to express months (Moon periods) and years (Sun periods) in whole days is rendered difficult on several grounds.

  (i) the real astronomical periods involve awkward fractions
 (ii) the solar period is not a neat multiple of the lunar period
(iii) the lunar period is variable from occasion to occasion (29.26 days to 29.80 days with a mean in the long run of about 29.53059 days)
(iv) though there are several lunar periods to choose between, the two most striking, the sidereal month and the synodic month, are different enough not to be confused with each other, whereas the several solar years are so much alike that it must have been difficult to establish early their differences and which was the most relevant for calendar-making.

On the last point let me remark on the situation for an Egyptian early in the third millennium BC, seen from our modern hindsight. The sidereal year was about 365.25636 days, the tropical year was about 365.24249965 days and the average intervals between the Sothic heliacal rising seen from Memphis was about 365.2507 days (I shall explain this a little later); 365.25 days is a fair enough average value but as Pope Gregory recognized not quite good enough as a match for the year of the seasons.

Twelve average lunar synodic months totalling about 354.367 days are near, but not quite near enough, to the several solar years I have mentioned. Some adjustment obviously has to be made if months and years are to be put together. Several compromises have been adopted. The first and perhaps most obvious is to let in an extra or intercalary month every now and then. This is what the Egyptians at first and the

Babylonians did and, perhaps following the Babylonians, what the Jews and the Greeks did. So also did the Hindus at first independently of and differently from the Babylonians but later on following the Babylonians' methods; the Chinese also adopted a later Babylonian pattern but whether independently or not is difficult to establish. This gets the months right in the sense that they are tied to the phases of the Moon though rounded to a whole day but the year is right only on average but never on any particular occasion—it is either too short by 10 or 11 days or too long by about 19 or 20 days. A calendar constructed on this principle is called luni-solar. The second compromise is to get the year right at least to the nearest whole day and to use schematic months about the length of the lunar synodic month but not tied to the phases of the Moon. This is what the Egyptians in their civil calendar, Julius Caesar and the later Hindus did. Such a calendar is called solar. The Republican Roman calendar used schematic months but instead of getting the year right on each occasion tried to get it right on average by use of an inter-calary month, thus having the defects of both a luni-solar and a solar calendar.

The Babylonians began the month on the day (which they regarded as beginning at sunset) on which there was a first visible crescent after sunset or which was the thirty-first day after the last sighting of the first crescent. As the intervals between one sighting and the next cannot be less than 29 days, the months were either 29 or 30 days in duration. As the lunar synodic period is a little over 29.53 days on average and as the first visible crescent occurs 1, 2 or even 3 days after conjunction for reasons set out in Chapter 2, the Babylonian months tended to be 29 or 30 days in rough alternation, with some 29 day months following each other and rather more 30 day months doing likewise. Twelve such months total 354 or 355 days, the latter occurring with about half the frequency of the former, that is some 11.2424 or some 10.2424 days less than the tropical year of about 365.2424 days.

When it became obvious that the year was ending about a month too early for the seasonal events deemed to occur about the end of the year or the end of the half year, an extra month was let in. We find Hammurabi in Babylon issuing a decree early in the second millennium:

> Since the year has a deficiency, let the month which is beginning be known as the second *Ululu*. But the tribute which is due in Babylon on the 25th day of *Tashritu* should be paid on the 25th day of the second *Ululu*.

Such an extra month would bring the total number of days in the year to 383, 384 (the most usual) or 385, depending on the total number of days in the preceding 12 months and on whether the extra month had 29 or 30 days.

Later the intercalation was made in accordance with some rule. We find the Greeks late in the first half of the first millennium, letting in the intercalary month in three years in a cycle of eight. It is not difficult to work out that the appropriate years in the cycle, the *octaeteris*, for intercalation would be the third, the fifth or the sixth, and the eighth. It was possible that the Babylonians may have been employing this rule, perhaps in less strict form, at about the same time or even earlier. The Babylonians were still setting their months by observation of the first crescent whereas the Greeks had moved to calculating it in advance (predictions being checked from time to time by observation). We know that the Athenians divided the month into three decades and counted the days forward in the first two but backwards from the end of the third (which of course sometimes had only 9 days in it). Clearly they could not have counted backwards unless they had calculated in advance the end of the month.

The *octaeteris* rule, however, did not get the months and the years quite in harmony. In 8 years, in 3 of which there was an intercalary month, there are 99 months which total about 2923.528 days, whereas 8 tropical years *circa* 750 BC total about 2921.943 days, a discrepancy of about 1.585 days. Such a discrepancy would after six cycles, that is 48 years, accumulate to about 8.5 days and after twelve cycles, that is 96 years, to about 19 days.

The Celts in Gaul, recorded in the Calendar of Coligney near the beginning of the Christian Era (see Powell, 1958), preserved in some fragments of bronze, a luni-solar calendar in which two intercalary months were introduced in a 5-year cycle. This rate of intercalation resulted in an excess of about 4.68 days in 5 years.

The Metonic cycle, named for the Greek astronomer Meton who enuniciated the rule in 432 BC but who may have been anticipated by the Babylonians, is a considerable improvement on the *octaeteris*. It uses a cycle of 19 years, 7 of which are embolistic or include an intercalary month. The cycle thus contains 235 months which total about 6939.688 days, whereas 19 tropical years *circa* 400 BC total about 6939.603 days. The difference of .084 days or about 2 hours accumulates to one day only after twelve cycles. Later both Kallippos and Hipparchos suggested more accurate versions involving sets of cycles some of 6,940 days (the nearest whole day to 6939.6 days) but a smaller number of only 6,939 days; this is essentially the system used by the Chinese from an early date.

Just as one can readily work out the points in the *octaeteris* where the embolistic years should occur, so one may do the same for the Metonic Cycle. They are, with alternatives at three points, the third, the fifth or the sixth, the eighth, the eleventh, the fourteenth or the fifteenth, the sixteenth or the seventeenth and the nineteenth years. I have calculated these positions on the assumption that the cumulative number of days from the beginning of the cycle should be within (29.53/2) days from the beginning of the year. As we shall see, other considerations producing much the same result obtained in Babylonia, in India and in China.

So far I have been talking in terms of average lunar synodic months. It will be more instructive to take a specific case. In column 1 of Table 4.1 are set out the dates and times of the lunar-solar conjunction as given in *The Nautical Almanac for the Year* 1973. From these values I have derived the durations of the several lunar synodic months which are set out in column 2. It will be noticed that the shortest synodic month in this series is 29 days 7 hours 5 minutes (or 29.295 days) in duration and the longest is 29 days 19 hours 12 minutes (or 29.80 days). The average is 29 days 11 hours 59 minutes (or 29.498 days, which is a little shorter than the long term average). I shall now explain the entries in column 3 headed 'Period in nearest cumulative day'.

The duration of the first synodic month is 29 days 17 hours 41 minutes, to which the nearest whole day is 30, the first entry in column 3. This first rounding has robbed 6 hours 19 minutes from the period to the third conjunction and so reduced the entry in column 2 of 29 days 14 hours 44 minutes to 29 days 8 hours 25 minutes, to which the nearest whole day is 29. This rounding leaves 8 hours 25 minutes to be added to the next synodic month of 29 days 11 hours 38 minutes, so it has to be rounded to 30 days, and so on. I have ignored here the varying intervals between the day of first visible crescent and the conjunction. Had allowance been made for them the Babylonian months would have varied a little from those set down in column 3, but the basic pattern would have been the same, namely months of 29 and 30 days in near alternation. In this example two rounded synodic months of 29 days occur in succession. In a year where the months tended to be longer than the long term average, a succession of two or even three 30-day months would occur.

Just as the day is divided into 24 hours (temporal or standard) or

month	Date and time of conjunction			Length of synodic month			Period in nearest cumulative day
	d.	h.	m.	d.	h.	m.	
Jan.	4	15	42				
				29	17	41	30
Feb.	3	9	23				
				29	14	44	29
Mar.	5	0	7				
				29	11	38	30
Apr.	3	11	45				
				29	9	10	29
May	2	20	55				
				29	7	39	30
Jun.	1	4	34				
				29	7	5	29
Jun.	30	11	39				
				29	7	20	29
Jul.	29	18	59				
				29	8	26	30
Aug.	28	3	25				
				29	10	29	29
Sep.	26	13	54				
				29	13	23	30
Oct.	26	3	17				
				29	16	38	29
Nov.	24	19	55				
				29	19	12	30
Dec.	24	15	7				

Table 4.1 Lunar conjunctions, synodic months and lunar months rounded to nearest cumulative whole day for AD 1973. The 12 synodic months total 353 days 23 hours and 25 minutes, and the 12 rounded 'months' total 354 days. The average synodic month is 29 days 11 hours 7 minutes or 29.498 days.

twelve *beru* or twelve *shih* or sixty *ghati* periods, all arbitrary, so the month has been divided in various ways by different calendar-makers. The most widespread division has perhaps been into the waxing and the waning halves of the lunar month. The Hindus from some early date divided the month into two *pakshas* (wings), the bright one while the Moon was waxing and increasingly illuminating the early night before people retired to their beds and the dark one while the Moon was waning and decreasingly illuminating the early night. The Celts in the Calendar of Coligney did likewise. In Babylonia *sabbatu*, the evening of the full Moon, and in Egypt, *smdt*, the day of the full Moon, seem to have been stressed, thus in effect dividing the month in two. In Greece stress was also placed on the *Noumenia* and the *Dichomenia*, the new and full Moon days. It is probable that the Roman *Kalendae* and *Idus* had a similar origin although they became fixed points in vestigial months in no way tied to the new Moon (or to the first visible crescent) and to the full Moon. The very wide concern with new Moon and full Moon frequently resulted in 'halves' of the month. There has often been superimposed on this twofold division a further twofold division related to the first and third quarters of the Moon. The evidence of this in Babylonia is fairly clear. There are also hints of a similar concern in Egypt where the seventh and the twenty-third days of the lunar month were called *dnit*, part day (see Parker, 1950, p. 11). It is also thought that the Roman *Nonae* may have originally been the day of the first quarter, (see Michels, 1967). Those who used a decimal number system were prone to divide the 29 or 30 lunar month or the schematic month of 30 days into thirds. Thus the Egyptians divided their schematic 30 months into three decades during which a given star, the decans, was the primary 'hour-marker'. However, after 360 days came the 5 epagomenal days to take up the first half of the next decade so that the next but one decade did not begin until the sixth day of *Thoth*, the first month. Thus the decades slipped in and out from the thirds of the actual schematic months. The Greeks also used decades but kept them tied to the lunar months, the first, middle and last decades. As the Greek lunar month was on almost half its occurrences only 29, the last 'decade' was often reduced to 9 days. The Chinese had a similar practice.

So far in this chapter I have been taking the year as determined by the apparent motions of the Sun somewhat for granted. I have mentioned the tropical year and the sidereal year, explained in Chapter 2, and the year based on the heliacal rising of *Sirius*, also called *Sothis* the Greek version of the Egyptian *Sophet*, as observed at Memphis in Egypt, and I have drawn attention to the similarity of the several periods. Let me repeat here that it was Hipparchos of the second century BC who is credited with the distinction between the sidereal and the tropical years, though Kidinnu, the Babylonian, is claimed to have anticipated him (but see Neugebauer, 1950). The sidereal year is defined as the interval between successive conjunctions of the Sun and some fixed star and it may be obtained by averaging the intervals between the heliacal risings of some star on or near the Ecliptic. The tropical year is defined as the interval between successive Spring Equinoxes (or any analogous pair of equinoxes or solstices). Instead of watching for the heliacal risings of say *Regulus, alpha Leonis* which is near the Ecliptic, the Egyptians seized on *Sirius, Sothis, Sophet, alpha Canis Majoris*, the brightest fixed star in our sky but well south of the Ecliptic. Its heliacal rising was, as shall be explained in a later chapter, for a time a harbinger of the all-important flooding of the Nile. Also the average interval between its successive heliacal risings as observed from Memphis is about 365.2507 days. It must have been extraordinarily difficult to get these several slightly different values right and to distinguish between them; indeed their very similarity may have had a confounding effect. Some other conventions did without doubt have a confounding effect. The Sumerian sexagesimal number system seems to have led those who used it to assume at first that the year *ought* to be 360 days (a fair enough compromise between 12 months of about 354.367 days and a tropical or sidereal year of about 365.25 days). There are hints that the Egyptians early harboured a similar preconception, looking perhaps for a neat multiple of 10, the base of their number system or a neat multiple of 30 which was the number of days in their schematic civil month.

I should like to report at this point two withdrawals from the task of trying to match the months and the year. The first was a Jewish group to whom we owe *The Book of Jubilees, Enoch* and the Dead Sea Scrolls. Its members were opposed to Moon-watching and to fixing time in accordance with the phases of the Moon. Instead, it would seem under the impress of the 7-day week, they settled for a year of 364 days (52 weeks exactly) divided into four seasons each consisting of 3 months of 30, 30 and 31 days or of 3 months of 30 days with an intercalated day at the end of each season. They were clearly poor astronomers: 364 days is a poor estimate of the tropical year and four sets of 91 days are distinctly inaccurate estimates of the seasons as measured from equinox to solstice and from solstice to equinox. They recognized that the seasons were out of step with what in their view they ought to have been but they attributed this to the sinfulness of man especially their neighbours (see Beckwith, 1970) as already reported.

I shall examine the second retreat from the problem more carefully.

Prior to Mohammed, the Arabians had been using some system of roughly alternating 29 and 30 day months based on observation of the first visible crescent with an intercalated thirteenth month every now and again as decided by a priestly caste, who seemed like the Roman pontifices to have abused their privilege, again possibly through a mixture of ignorance and cunning. Mohammed proscribed any further intercalation and instituted a calendar based primarily on calculation of the prospective first visible crescent. The months except for the twelfth alternated between 29 and 30 days, as may be seen in Table 4.2. The twelfth month, *Dul Hija* had on a fixed pattern either 29 days (on nineteen occasions) or 30 days (in the remaining 11 years in a 30-year cycle). This schematization resulted in 19 years of 354 days and 11 of 355 days with an average of 354.36 days for the year and 29.5305 days for the month. The latter is only a little less than 7.595 seconds shorter than our modern estimate of the average lunar synodic month.

The Mohammedan calendar is one of the few remaining purely lunar calendars. It gets the lunar months approximately right but ignores the solar year. There are grounds for believing that this is the way luni-solar and most solar calendars began. In that case the Mohammedan calendar is an atavistic one.

When Mohammed in the early seventh century AD, established his calendar with years averaging 354.36 days, the tropical year was about 365.24227 days in length. Hence his shorter year worked its way forward through the tropical year or the year of the seasons in about 33 tropical years. In 1967 the 1st day of *Muharran* began after sunset on our Gregorian 12 April, 16 years earlier it occurred on our 3 October.

Though the calendar presented in Table 4.2 is clearly one based on calculations rather than observations of the first visible crescent, rural Mohammedans in almost every country have tended to use a variant of it based on observation. In particular, they have paid attention to the first visible crescent following *Ramadan*, the month of fasting.

This purely lunar calendar is in widespread use from North Africa, through much of Central Africa, most of the Middle East, in Southern Asia and in Southeast Asia, that is wherever Mohammedanism is to be found. In Persia and in India it runs alongside other calendars. It has carried with it the 7-day week wherever it has gone.

I have so far referred to approximate lunar synodic months tied to the phases of the Moon and to schematic or vestigial months approximating the lunar synodic month but not tied to the lunar phases. I now wish to draw attention to what may be called 'solar months' as indeed

1. Maharran (30 days)	7. Rajab (30 days)
2. Safar (29 days)	8. Shaban (29 days)
3. Rabi-ul-avval (30 days)	9. Ramadan (30 days)
4. Rabi-al-akhir (29 days)	10. Shavvai (29 days)
5. Jami-ul-avval (30 days)	11. Dul Kada (30 days)
6. Jami-ul-akhir (29 days)	12. Dul Hijja (29 or 30 days)

Table 4.2 The Mohammedan near lunar months. All but *Dul Hijja* have a fixed duration; it has 29 days in 19 years in a cycle of 30 years, and 30 days in 11 of these years. The years as a consequence total 354 (on nineteen occasions) and 355 (on eleven occasions) and average 354.36 days, which is very close to the average of 12 lunar synodic months.

the Hindus call them. They are the periods rounded to the nearest whole day required by the Sun to traverse a 30° segment of the Zodiac, that is a Sign. As we saw in Chapter 2, this may be as short a period as 29.40 days (the passage through Capricorn), when the Earth is in the neighbourhood of perihelion and as long as 31.48 days (the passage through Cancer), when it is in the neighbourhood of aphelion. Twelve such 'months' equal the tropical year if allowance is made for the rounding to whole days. The practice of noting the periods between the passage of the Sun into one and into the next Sign is Babylonian though whether the Babylonians applied the term 'month' to the period I do not know. The very ancient Chinese practice of marking off the periods called *chhi*, namely the period taken by the Sun to traverse a 15° segment of the Celestial Equator is similar in principle though probably independent in origin (see Needham, 1959).

It may be appropriate here to remark on differences in Middle Eastern (Babylonian, Greek, Egyptian, Persian and by inheritance Indian) astronomical conventions and Chinese conventions. In the occident early observations were made primarily in respect of the horizon—settings and risings—and where located within the Celestial Sphere in relation to the Ecliptic, the Sun's apparent path among the fixed stars. In China from very early times observations were made in respect of the meridian, the imaginary line passing through the zenith and the North Celestial pole. Celestial positions were related to the Equator (see de Saussure, 1919b and Needham, 1959). Modern astronomy uses both the ecliptic and the polar-equatorial systems, though the latter is regarded as the basic one. In it, two celestial bodies are regarded as having the same east-west longitude (called Right Ascension) if they cross the meridian together. Their location in the north-south latitude (called Declination) is measured in degrees, north or south, from the Celestial Equator. The Right Ascension (expressed in hours and minutes after the meridian crossing of the First Point of Aries) and the Declination (expressed in degrees of angle) of a fixed star are both affected by the precession of the equinoxes. In the alternative system, the ancient occidental one, longitude and latitude, both so-called in modern astronomy, are measured in degrees of angle along and from the Ecliptic respectively. Latitude is not affected by the precession of the equinoxes. Longitude is so affected only in so far as it is measured from the First Point of Aries. After the Babylonians had replaced the Zodiacal constellations, unequal in extent, with the Zodiacal Signs, all 30° in extent along the Ecliptic, they tended to express longitude in terms of so many degrees within a Sign, e.g., Regulus was about 29° within the Sign *Leo* in AD 1900 and about 1° within that Sign in 100 BC, the difference being the result of precession. Throughout this period, its latitude has been about 1° north of the Ecliptic.

The use of longitude along and latitude from the Ecliptic endured in the West until late medieval times, whereafter it was replaced for the principal plotting of star locations by the convention related to the Equator. It is amusing to see some late medieval star lists (see Skeat, 1872) using one convention for 'longitude' and the other for 'latitude' or *vice versa*.

5/SOME CIRCLES OF STARS

Before I proceed to the examination of individual calendars I wish to discuss further some of the circles of stars adopted in the Near East, in India and the Far East in ancient times for purposes of time-reckoning or for season-marking. Hesiod in his *Works and Days* provides an oft-cited example of the use of a star or star group as a seasonal-marker.

> When the Pleiades, the daughters of Atlas are rising, begin your harvest and your ploughing when they are going to set. Forty nights and days they are hidden and appear again when first you sharpen your sickle (Evelyn-White's translation)

The rising referred to here is the heliacal rising of the Pleiades, the first visible rising before sunrise after the period of invisibility while this star group was in near conjunction with the Sun. *Circa* 700 BC at the latitude where Hesiod lived in Boeotia, this would have occurred on or about 20 May (Julian) according to some extrapolations I have made from data given by Bickerman. The period of invisibility was according to other extrapolations from these data about 45 days, not the forty claimed by Hesiod.

Before I proceed further I should like to explain a few conventions concerning the naming of stars and constellations. From very early times individual stars have been given personal names, such as *Sophet* so named by the Egyptians but which the Greeks rendered as *Sothis*, though they themselves called it *Seirios*, the scorcher, perhaps because its heliacal rising occurred in the hot summer-time; the Latinized form of the Greek name was *Sirius*, our name. In Mesopotamia, it was called the arrow, *gag. si. sa*, or perhaps the tip of the arrow, projecting from *ban*, the bow, made up by a number of other stars we regard as constituting *Canis Major*. We also call it *alpha Canis Majoris*, in accordance with a convention I shall explain later.

The name of the brightest star in the constellation *Leo* provides another interesting example (see Allen, 1899). It is now known as *Regulus*, less often as *Cor Leonis*, and also as *alpha Leonis*. The Baby-

50

lonians called it *Sharru*, the King, Ptolemy called it *Basiliskos*, the Little King and Roman writers *Rex*, the King. Arab astronomers called it *Qalb al Asad*, the heart of the lion, probably because of its position in the constellation *Leo*. This Arabic name appears in corrupted form in medieval Europe as *Calbalezed*, *Galbaiced* and so on. Copernicus called it *Regulus*, the Latin diminutive of *Rex*.

From very early times groups of stars were taken to represent some object, human, animal or artefact, which to our eyes often require a considerable stretch of the imagination. I can see with no difficulty the Scorpion, Orion the hunter, the Bull and perhaps a few other constellations. I regard most constellations as arbitrary *gestalten*. Therefore, I applaud the convention adopted by international agreement among modern astronomers to fence off, often with somewhat jagged boundaries, the constellations in terms of meridians of Right Ascension and parallels of Declination (both oriented to the Celestial Equator and the Celestial Poles). With the adoption of this convention, the somewhat earlier convention of giving the brightest stars in the constellation a Greek letter designation usually in descending order of brightness has been adopted and when the Greek alphabet has been exhausted an Arabic number. In a few cases a Greek letter with a numeral subscript has been used, for instance in the stars making up the lion-skin shield of *Orion*, which are called pi_1, pi_2, pi_3 *Orionis* and so on.

Perhaps the earliest circle of stars on which we have evidence involves four constellations lying roughly along the Ecliptic and about 90° of longitude between centres or leading edges. Their heliacal risings would have marked the beginnings of the four seasons *circa* 4000 BC for the Mesopotamians who used them. According to Hartner they were the Bull's Jaw, the Lion (Gössmann says it may have been the Great Dog), the Scorpion and the Ibex (later the Moufflon in Persia). The Bull's Jaw, it seems, consisted of the Hyades as the bull's head with *Aldebaran* (*alpha Tauri*) as a bright shining eye and two crumpled horns, the southern one formed by the stars we use to define Orion's lion-skin shield and the western one formed by some stars in our *Taurus* ending with the Pleiades. I shall say something more about this truncated bull later. The Lion was much the same as our *Leo* though *beta Virginis* may have marked his hindfoot and some stars to the west his forelegs. The Scorpion was much as we see it, tail raised and sting pointing forward about to strike, but its fore-claws extended to our *alpha* and *beta Librae*, marking for us the pans of the Balance. The Ibex was seen as a magnificent specimen of the *Capridae* family with great backward sweeping horns as often depicted on early vases and seals. It had our *Capricornus* as its hindquarters, our *Aquarius* as head, neck and forelegs and some stars to the north of the two as the pair of great backward sweeping curved horns (see Hartner, 1965).

Sometime later the Egyptians used a rough circle of 36 stars, called by the Greeks the *decans*, perhaps first for marking out the set of 10 days, a third of the 30-day civil month and perhaps later the 'hours' of the night. Apart from *Sirius* (*alpha Canis Majoris*) and *Orion* (or some star or stars in that constellation) we don't know the identity of these stars. Some general things are known or conjectured about them. If they were to serve the purposes they are said to have served they would have been about 10° in longitude apart, in which case the 'hours' marked off by their successive risings and/or settings would have been about 40 of our minutes. Neugebauer and Parker (1969, pp. 97–100) claim that all of them shared, at least approximately, *Sirius'* 70 days of invisibility, the period of embalming between death, at the heliacal setting, and resurrection, at the heliacal rising. They claim on this basis that they lay in a band south of but roughly parallel to the Ecliptic.

The Mesopotamians, at about the same time as the Egyptians were using their 36 decans, also had a set of 36 stars which at first were probably quite differently arranged. In the *Epic of Creation* (see Langdon, 1923) it is said that for the 12 months, Marduk placed three stars each. It would seem that these stars had their heliacal risings during the month in the normal set of twelve as marked out by the phases of the Moon. These stars lay in three rough bands (see van der Waerden, 1949), those in the north being in Enlil's Way, those nearest the Celestial Equator being in Anu's Way and those in the south being in Ea's Way. Anu, Enlil and Ea were the gods of the heavens, of the air and of water (and perhaps of the earth) respectively. The Sun spent about 3 months, the cold and watery ones, in Ea's Way, about 3, the hot and dry ones, in Enlil's Way and two sets of about 3, the stormy and windy ones, in Anu's Way. It is probable that these twelve sets of three stars or star groups had a bearing on the later choice of twelve zodiacal constellations to which I shall devote a good deal of attention later. It also seems that the original 36 stars later gave way to another 36 roughly in an Ecliptic circle serving time-reckoning functions rather like the Egyptian decans (see van der Waerden, 1949).

Further east and probably later than the Egyptian decans and the original Mesopotamian 36 stars allotted to the three ways, we find the two related systems of 27, sometimes 28, Hindu *nakshatra* stars or star groups and of 28 Chinese *hsiu* stars. Later still we find the 28 Arabian *Al Manazil* almost certainly derived from the Indian *nakshatra* stars. All are rough circles of stars, on average about 13° apart and related in a rough way to the Moon's change of position night by night on its eastward journey through the fixed stars. Their number, 27 or 28, is clearly related to the Moon's average sidereal period of about 27.32 days. The Hindus thought of the *nakshatra* stars as the companions or brides of the Moon, the Chinese regarded the *hsiu* stars as the places of the Moon and the Arabic *Al Manazil* are the inns of the Moon. In India the Moon, *Chandra*, as in Babylonia, *Sin*, was regarded as male. In neither the Hindu and the Arabian system nor in the Chinese system do the designated stars or star groups mark the nightly resting places of the Moon. First, there could be such nightly resting places only if the lunar sidereal month consisted of a whole number of days, say 27 or 28 rather than 27.32 on average. Second, granted this first condition, the companions, palaces or inns would have to be fairly evenly spaced. The *nakshatra* are nearer to an even spacing, except when the twenty-eighth is added, than the *hsiu* but they are both rather unevenly spaced (see de Saussure, 1919a). The spacing of the *hsiu* stars varies from a few degrees to as much as 30° plus, it would seem so that circumpolars on the same meridian could be used as a northern protractor necessarily unevenly calibrated but visible in full on any clear night. I have compared the *nakshatra* stars as identified by Renou and Filliozat with the *hsiu* stars as identified by Needham. About one-third are identical, about one-third are neighbours and about one-third are remote from one another. Further the *nakshatra* lie roughly along the Ecliptic whereas the *hsiu* lie roughly along the celestial Equator, a point made by both de Saussure (1919a) and Needham (1959). It is also worth nothing that *hsiu* stars separated by fourteen places are approximately 180° in Right Ascension apart.

Early in the first millennium AD the Hindus substituted 27 even segments of the Ecliptic, each 13°20′ in extent and transferred both the generic name *nakshatra* and the individual *nakshatra* star names to them. Each of these schematic *nakshatra* segments was divided into four *pada*, a Sanskrit word cognate with the Latin *pes* and English 'foot', each 3°20′ in extent. Further, the name of the schematic *nakshatra* segments in which the full Moon usually occurred was transferred first to the lunar and later to the overlapping solar month.

I wish to explore a little more thoroughly the development of the twelve zodiacal constellations and of the later schematic twelve zodiacal signs, each 30° in extent. Both the constellations and the signs are almost certainly of Mesopotamian (probably Babylonian) origin, the constellations going back to the second millennium BC (see van der Waerden, 1949, and Neugebauer, 1969). In what follows I am trying to piece together a great deal of incomplete evidence available to me only through secondary sources as I cannot read the cuneiform texts and can only with difficulty consult the several dictionaries, e.g., Gössmann (1950), the Chicago *Assyrian Dictionary* and Meissner's *Akkadisches Handwörterbuch* (1965), available to me and then only in so far as Roman transliteration is used. Gössmann (1950), Ungnad (1941–4), van der Waerden (1949), Sachs (1952a) and Neugebauer (especially 1969) have been of great value.

I shall in the case of each zodiacal constellation give the Sumerian and the Akkadian names and their meanings. I shall record the Sumerian name or names in capitals (omitting the prefix MUL, star) and the Akkadian in minuscules. The existence of a Sumerian name does not necessarily mean a Sumerian bestowal. It seems that the Akkadian-speaking scribes of Babylonia and Assyria often used Sumerian words for technical and other serious matters as we have tended to turn to Latin and to Greek. I shall add the Greek name or names, usually translations of the Mesopotamian and the Latin and Sanskrit names usually translations of the Greek. I shall also try to indicate the composition of the constellation where there seems to be reasonable evidence on the matter and the pictorial representation. The pictorial representations which were popular in medieval and early modern times, e.g., Dürer's engraving of 1515 and Bayer's illustrations in his seventeenth century *Uranometria*, go back to Hellenistic times, e.g., the representations on the ceiling and walls of the temple of Hathor at Denderah in Egypt (see Boll, 1903 and Maspero, 1914) and the drawings in a Hellenistic document, epoch unspecified, reproduced by Boll and Gundel. Few Mesopotamian representations, if the practice were common, remain to us. However, some clues may be provided by the carvings on Mesopotamian boundary stones (see King 1912, and van der Waerden, 1953). In addition to representations at the top of the stones of the Sun (*Shamash*), the Moon (*Sin*) and a large star, probably Venus (*Ishtar*), are a great variety of other figures which do not necessarily have celestial reference though they are almost certainly gods, goddesses and other ruling spirits.

I shall begin with *Taurus* the heliacal rising of which would have marked the opening of Spring and the year when the twelve zodiacal constellations were being built up from the original four seasonal markers already described.

Taurus, the bull

It would seem that in the early third millennium BC the Sumerian name was *IS.LI.E.* (later in Akkadian, *issu.sa.le*), the bull's jaw. I have already described the abbreviated constellation seen as a bull's head with two crumpled horns. The Pleiades seen as the tip of the western horn were called *MUL.MUL* meaning either the stars or the star *par excellence*. Later we find the Pleiades being called *zappu*, the hair, perhaps a reference to the bull's mane, though it may refer to the hazy appearance of this asterism when near the horizon. The Greeks later called it *Kometes*, the long-haired, a name they also used for hazy comets. If the Pleiades were seen as marking the mane, the tips of the horns would have been shifted to *beta* and *zeta Tauri*, that is marking a pair of protruding horns as in late ancient representations. Perhaps as in later conceptions shoulder and forelegs were seen to the west and south of the Pleiades, but still a truncated bull cut off behind the shoulders as is suggested by representations on early vases and seals. The name changed to *GU.UD.AN.NA* and *alap.same*, the bull of heaven. In the Denderah ceiling a whole bull is shown, whereas in the Boll and Gundel pictures the bull is cut off behind the shoulders as in most later representations, emerging from a cloud or swimming in the sea.

I suggest that the notion of the truncated bull to be seen in the Boll and Gundel pictures, most medieval representations, in Dürer's engraving and Bayer's illustrations go back to an incident in the Mesopotamian *Epic of Gilgamesh*. Ishtar, the goddess of love and war, represented in the sky by the planet Venus, angered by Gilgamesh's rejection of her advances to him, arranged for the bull of heaven to devastate the denizens of the Earth. At his first snort, a hundred died and successive snorts resulted in multiples of a hundred deaths. Gilgamesh, the king of Uruk shortly after the Flood, and his feral friend Enkidu slew the bull of heaven and cut out his heart which they presented to Shamash, the Sun-god and their protector. Ishtar severely rebuked them for their action but Enkidu in defiance, cut off the bull's hind leg (or another member according to some translators), flung it at Ishtar saying that he wished he could do likewise with her entrails.

Sometimes in Mesopotamia the name of the bull-of-heaven was

55

abbreviated to the bull and so it was translated into Greek, *Tauros* and thence in Latin, *Taurus* and later Sanskrit, *Vrishabha*, the bull.

Gemini, the twins

The Mesopotamian names were *MAS.TAB.BA.GAL.GAL* and *masu. rabati*, the great twins of heaven. These names may have been applied only to *alpha* and *beta Geminorum*, *Castor* and *Pollux*, and not to the two straggling lines of stars descending southwest from these two stars. Another pair of stars lower in the two lines, possibly *zeta* and *lambda* or *iota* and *nu Geminorum* (the experts disagree), was called *MAS.TAB.BA.TUR.TUR*, the small twins.

In the Denderah ceiling a pair of erect human figures are shown, one possibly female and the other male standing feet apart. This feet apart posture may have been suggested by the obvious bifurcation of the lower stars, straggling down from *Castor*. The Boll and Gundel pictures show a pair of standing human figures whereas Dürer's later engraving shows a pair of entwined naked boyish figures. I have heard of Renaissance or early modern representations of a more intimately entwined male and female. Both Boll and Gundel (1937), and Allen (1899) report a number of unlike-sex twins. Allen also reports that the straggling lines of stars were called the piles of bricks and suggests, implausibly to my mind, that this notion is related to Romulus and Remus, the fratricidal twins who founded Rome. Langdon claims that the heliacal rising of *Gemini* was once associated in Mesopotamia with the month of brick-making.

The Greek *Didymoi*, the Latin *Gemini* and the Sanskrit *Mithuna*, all mean the twins.

Cancer, the crab

This rather formless set of dim stars was called *NAN.GAR* and *kusu*, some sort of animal, probably aquatic, and later *AL.LUL* and *allutu*, the crab. Later part of it was and is still called *Praesepe*, Latin for the manager or perhaps the bee-hive. The whole thing might well be thought of as a swarm of bees. The multi-legged round creature represented on the Denderah ceiling is a fair enough representation of the rather formless constellation whereas the Boll and Gundel picture of a crab and Dürer's picture of a lobster have little justification in the pattern of the stars themselves.

The Greek *Karkinos*, the Latin *Cancer* and the Sanskrit *Karka*, all mean the crab.

Leo, the lion

The Mesopotamian *UR.GU.LA*, sometimes abbreviated to *UR.A*. or *A*, perhaps the great dog or possibly the lion (Gössmann, 1950) and *nesu*, the lion, was seen according to Hartner (1965), to Gössmann and to van der Waerden (1953) much as we see *Leo*. *Beta Virginis* was probably regarded as a hind foot of the lion and some stars to the west of our constellation may have been seen as the forelegs. Allen (1899) claims that later the Arabs saw *Castor* and *Pollux* as two points in one foreleg and *Procyon, alpha Canis Minoris*, as a point in the other. Chaucer in *The Squire's Tale* refers to the gentle Leo, the royal beast, ascending with his Aldiran. In near contemporary astrolabe star lists is a star Aldiran (also spelled Aldiraan and Aldirun) said to be *in fronte leonis*. The name is almost certainly a corruption of the Arabic *Al Dhira'an*, meaning the arms or the forelegs. In one list it is given a position (never very accurate in these lists) about midway between *theta* and *zeta Hydrae* (Skeat, 1872).

The Greek *Leon*, the Latin *Leo* and the Sanskrit *Simha*, all mean the lion.

Virgo, the virgin

This somewhat sprawling set of stars lying roughly along the Ecliptic was called *AB.SIN* and *absinnu*, the furrow. Gössmann says that *Spica,alpha Virginis*, and the stars in our *Virgo* to the east were regarded as an ear of grain and that the stars to the west other than *beta Virginis* (the hind foot of the lion) as a cluster of date palm flowers. Grain and dates were the two principal products of the Mesopotamian furrow. Our name *Spica* is a Latin word for an ear of grain. Langdon (1935) and van der Waerden (1953) claim that the Mesopotamian representation of *absinnu* became a fertility goddess. Goddesses were usually shown as winged (see King). Langdon reports a winged goddess with an ear of wheat in one hand and a date flower in the other and van der Waerden reproduces a female figure standing in what may be furrow and holding a stalk of wheat. In the Denderah ceiling the constellation is represented as a female figure holding in one hand an ear of grain. In the Boll and Gundel pictures a winged female figure is shown, sometimes lying along the Ecliptic, sometimes holding the scales, the next zodiacal constellation in her hand, but in one picture what may be a grain stalk or a frond.

The Greeks and Romans tended to identify this figure with Demeter (Ceres), the goddess of the fertility of the Earth. In medieval Europe, the winged, often haloed, female figure, sometimes with an ear of grain in one hand and a date palm in the other, was identified with the Virgin Mary.

The Greek *Parthenos*, the Latin *Virgo* and the Sanskrit *Kanya* all mean virgin. Though the name *absinnu*, the furrow, the identification with the ear of grain and the cluster of date flowers and perhaps the representation as a winged goddess of fertility all seem to have originated in Mesopotamia, I suspect the switch from actual to potential fertility may have been Greek, even though it may have occurred in Mesopotamia after the Greek conquest (see Gössmann, 1950). Van der Waerden (1953) argues for a pure Mesopotamian origin.

Libra, the weighing scales

When *alpha* and *beta Librae* ceased to be the claws of the older Scorpion, the Mesopotamian names *SIS.RIN* or *ZIB.BA.AN.NA* and *zibanitu*, the weighing scales, were given to this constellation. In the Denderah ceiling and in the Boll and Gundel pictures, it is represented by a balance—fulcrum, beam and suspended pans. In the Boll and Gundel pictures the scales are once shown as held by *Virgo* and once by another female figure.

In Greek the name was either *Chelai*, the claws, or *Zugon*, the beam or the balance. The Latin *Libra* means the weighing scales whereas the Sanskrit *Tula* means the beam (of the balance).

Scorpio, *Scorpius*, the scorpion

GIR.TAB and *agrabu* or *zuqaqipu* mean the scorpion. This constellation looks like the creature for which it is named. There are several carvings of a scorpion in the same posture, tail raised and sting pointing forward on Mesopotamian boundary stones (see King, 1912). The representations in the Denderah ceiling and in the Boll and Gundel pictures show a more passive scorpion.

Having always, as a southern hemisphere observer, seen this aptly named constellation right way up, I was startled once when flying north of the equator to wake up early in the morning to see the unfortunate creature on its back. No wonder the northern ancients considered that the following Sagittarius had Scorpio at his mercy.

The Greek *Skorpios*, the Latin *Scorpio* and *Scorpius*, and the Sanskrit *Vriscika* all mean the scorpion.

Sagittarius, the archer

This constellation was called *PA.BIL.SAG*, a word of uncertain meaning, though Gössmann suggests 'the arrow shooter'. Langdon gives as alternative and perhaps later names *US* and *redu*, the soldier. In the Denderah ceiling it is represented as a winged bow-drawing centaur almost identical with some of the Mesopotamian boundary-stone figures and in the Boll and Gundel pictures it is shown either as a bow-drawing centaur or as a bow-drawing satyr. On the Mesopotamian boundary stones reported by King there is also a bow-drawing half-man, half-scorpion. Boll reproduces a figure which I take to be Hellenistic of an archer with tight-fitting cap, man down to the waist topping the rump, tail and hind legs of a horse. This arrow shooting monster was usually thought of as aiming at the scorpion just ahead of him in remembrance of a scorpion sting which in myth had brought about the centaur's demise.

The Greek *Toxotis* and the Latin *Sagittarius* mean the archer, whereas the Sanskrit *Dhanus* means the bow, a notion used in the Mesopotamian *ban* for a substantial part of *Canis Major*.

Capricornus, the goat-horned

When this constellation, originally the hind quarters of the Ibex, was given separate identity it was called *SUHUR.MAS* and *suhur.massu*, the fish-goat. King reports a number of fish-goats on Mesopotamian boundary stones; they appear as recumbent goats with hind quarters usually hidden by a shrine or tabernacle. The Denderah ceiling and the Boll and Gundel pictures show a monster half-goat, half-fish which became the standard representation, for example in Dürer's engraving of AD 1515.

The Greek *Aigokeros* and the Latin *Capricornus* mean the goat-horned one, whereas the Sanskrit *Makara* means the sea-monster.

Aquarius, the water-carrier

Originally the head and forequarters of the Ibex, when given separate identity this constellation was called *GU.LA*, a word of uncertain meaning, though Gössmann suggests that it may have been 'the great man' or 'the giant'. He also claims that it was represented as a man with an upturned water cask or urn from which water streamed. It is so represented in the Denderah ceiling, almost identical with some boundary-stone figures and in the Boll and Gundel pictures. Ungnad (1941–4) suggests that its Akkadian name may have been *qu.hasbu*, the threads (or streams) of an urn. Part of the constellation is still called the Water Pot. The Denderah ceiling and many later representations show the water streaming down to the mouth of the Southern fish. The brightest star in the latter constellation is Fomulhaut a corruption of the Arabic *Fum al Hut*, the mouth of the fish.

The Greek *Hydrochoos* means the water pourer, the Latin *Aquarius* means the water-carrier whereas the Sanskrit *Kumbha* means the urn, a name applied in the West to part of the constellation.

Pisces, the fishes

The Mesopotamian names were *KUN.MES* or *ZIB.ME* and *zibbati*, the tails, or *DUR.NU.NU* and *rikis.nunu*, the fish-cord. The Denderah ceiling and the Boll and Gundel pictures show two fish tied by the tails. In the Denderah ceiling the cord tying the two fish is vee-shaped, the apex being no doubt at *alpha Piscium*. Lying between the two fish in that representation is a rectangle with wavy lines, suggesting water, across it. This is our Square of Pegasus marked out by *alpha Andromedae* and *beta*, *gamma* and *delta Pegasi*. It was called in Mesopotamia *IKU*, the field and in the Denderah representation it was probably the flooded field. The Square of Pegasus was used in Mesopotamia as an alternative to the fish-tails as a mile-post for the Sun's progress among the fixed stars. Van der Waerden (1949) shows the probable composition of the two fish tied by the tails, also called 'the swallow', larger fish than our two as they embrace some stars in our *Andromeda* and in our *Pegasus*.

The Greek *Ichthyes*, the Latin *Pisces* and the Sanskrit *Mina*, all mean the fishes.

The fish-goat, the giant emptying his water-cask and the two fish suggest three rainy months or at least months of flood in the lower reaches of the Euphrates-Tigris river system. These are the months which the Sun originally spent in water god Ea's Way.

Aries, the ram

Quite early in Mesopotamia this constellation was called *LU.HUN.GA* (often abbreviated to *LU*, to *HUN.GA* and to *HUN*) and *agru*, the hired farm-worker. Many early Mesopotamian and Persian seals and vases show the hireling beneath his plough, *APIN*, our Triangulum plus *gamma Andromedas* and behind the truncated bull. Sometimes he is shown applying a starry goad to the bull, no doubt prompting the latter's heliacal rising, which had early marked the onset of Spring, so that the diligent worker could get on with his round of agrarian duties (see Hartner, 1965).

In the Denderah ceiling, in the Boll and Gundel pictures and in other early representations, the constellation is shown as a ram, usually recumbent and once with a surcingle around it just behind the shoulders.

It is thought that the transformation of the hired farm-worker into the ram occurred in Mesopotamia. Langdon (1935) suggests that as this constellation was in Ea's Way and as a ram was long associated with Ea (perhaps a sacrificial ram akin to the Jewish springtime Pascal lamb) the ram came to be associated with this later Spring-marking constellation. Ungnad (1941–4) has a different suggestion. There were two homophones written with different cuneiform characters. One was *LU* the abbreviation of *LU.HUN.GA* and so of *agru*, the other was LU and *immeru*, the sheep. I find Ungnad's suggestion the more plausible.

The Greek *Krios*, the Latin *Aries* and the Sanskrit *Mesha*, all mean the ram.

It would seem that with three possible exceptions namely *absinnu*, *GU.LA* and *agru*, the Mesopotamian names were translated first into Greek and from Greek independently into Latin and with a few variations into Sanskrit. There is evidence that the Indians, perhaps in Dravidian rather than Aryan-speaking regions, used corruptions rather than translations of the Greek names, for example *Tavuri* from *Tauros*, *Leya* from *Leon*, *Pathena* from *Parthenos* and *Kreya* from *Krios* (see Dreyer, 1953).

One may speculate on the division of the zodiac into twelve constellations. Four related matters may be considered. First, 12 lunar months occurred more frequently than 13 in the course of a solar year of the seasons so the Sun spent about a month in each constellation (see van der Waerden, 1949). Second, in the old Mesopotamian system of 36 stars there were twelve sets of three stars, with the Sun spending about 3 months in Ea's Way, two sets of about 3 months in Anu's Way and about 3 months in Enlil's Way. Third, the six constellations which usually rose during the course of a night would serve to mark out the six 2-hour periods, each a *beru*, into which it was divided. Fourth, twelve is a neat fraction in the Mesopotamian sexagesimal number system.

So far I have been discussing the zodiacal constellations which were of unequal Ecliptic extents, *absinnu* being quite long, say over 35° and *agru* quite short, say about 20° of longitude. About 400 BC when Babylonian astronomy was becoming more quantitative and precise, the division into twelfths was schematized into twelve equal signs each 30° in extent (see Neugebauer, 1969). This schematization may have begun as early as 700 BC (see van der Waerden, 1953). Each sign contained a zodiacal constellation usually *in toto* and was given the same name. This was highly convenient for the Hellenistic astronomers who adopted the Babylonian convention of expressing longitudes as so many degrees in such and such a sign. The Greeks used the letters of their alphabet supplemented by some archaic alphabetic signs as numerals, so the smaller the numbers used the better.

When late in the second century BC Hipparchos demonstrated the precession of the equinoxes it became evident that if the spring crossing of the Equator by the Sun were to be regarded as the First Point of Aries, the zodiacal constellations were slowly slipping eastward out of the like-named signs. As pointed out in Chapter 2, the sign *Aries* now contains the constellation *Pisces*, the constellation *Aries* being in the sign *Taurus*. Modern astronomy which changed from longitude and latitude relative to the Ecliptic to Right Ascension and Declination relative to the Equator as its positional reference frame has no use for the signs which have been preserved largely by astrology; the planets are presumed to exercise different influences in different signs, although originally in different zodiacal constellations.

When the Indians adopted the twelvefold division of the Ecliptic into signs they tried for some calendrical purposes to freeze the effect of precession to an epoch early in the first millennium AD. They also equated the signs to nine *pada*, the quarters of the schematic *nakshatra* segments of the Ecliptic. When the Buddhist monks took the signs of the zodiac from India to China, *circa* AD 600, the Chinese adopted a completely different set of twelve animal names which had been in use for a number of twelve unit cycles, for example of days, of months and of years. They also related the signs to pairs of the 15° segments of the Equator which were used to mark off the twenty-four *chhi* periods of 15 or 16 days (see Needham, 1959 on both these points).

6/THE EGYPTIAN CALENDARS

It will be all too easy here for a foolish amateur to rush in where learned experts seem unhesitant to tread. The experts have been working diligently and ingeniously for well over a century trying to piece together numerous scraps of evidence derived from many periods of time extending over more than three millennia from about 3000 BC and to provide a coherent and conclusive account of ancient Egyptian calendrical practices. Though there is much that must still be regarded as being in doubt, several points seem to be reasonably well established. We know most about the Egyptian civil calendar with its 'vague' or schematic year of 365 days, consisting of 12 schematic months, not tied to the phases of the Moon, plus 5 supplementary or epagomenal days outside the months. There was nothing vague in the ordinary sense about the Egyptian civil year. We derive the term 'vague' from the Latin *annus vagus*, meaning the wandering year. The evidence on the late schematic luni-solar calendar has been convincingly interpreted by Parker (1950). I have little doubt about Parker's evidence on the existence of the earlier luni-solar calendar, almost certainly preceding the civil calendar, but I have some doubts about Parker's detailed conclusions in respect of it; nevertheless I shall rely heavily on his contentions.

Let me begin with the civil calendar which may have been introduced in the early part of the third millennium BC, if not earlier, and which endured unchanged to the end of the dynastic period (that is, to about the beginning of the Christian era) and continued in modified form among the Copts (in both Egypt and Ethiopia), the Persians and the Parsees in India up to the present day. I shall leave until later some controversial questions in relation to it. As I have stated, it consisted of 365 days, near to but not quite near enough to the tropical year of almost 365.25 days. Not only was this year schematic but also the 12 months in it were schematic. The months were each 30 days in duration, near to the 29 or 30 days of the strict lunar month but not tied to the cycle of phases of the Moon. To round these 360 days out to 365 days, there were 5 epagomenal days outside the months, placed between successive 12 months and at least late in the piece regarded as the last 5 days of the year.

Days were numbered forward in the months, and though in inscriptions the months were given numbers within a season, it is probable that they always had names, names which changed with changing emphasis on the festivals which occurred within them. The months were grouped in fours into three seasons, named as far as I can make out, Inundation, Cultivation (or perhaps literally 'the showing forth' either in relation to the land as the flood receded or in relation to the growth of plants) and the Harvest (or perhaps literally 'the deficiency' referring to the low water level in the lower Nile). The late names, say from 1500 BC or later, of the months were as follows:

Inundation	Cultivation	Harvest
1. *Thoth*	1. *Tybi*	1. *Pechons*
2. *Phaophi*	2. *Mechir*	2. *Payni*
3. *Athyr*	3. *Phamenoth*	3. *Epiphi*
4. *Choiak*	4. *Pharmuthi*	4. *Mesore*

It is possible that the concept of three seasons preceded the institution of the civil calendar with its 365-day year and that it was based on the behaviour of the Nile, about which I shall have a lot more to say later. Though the solar year of about 365.25 days has a marked bearing on the terrestrial year of the seasons, this effect may have been less obvious in the lower Nile Valley than in some other regions where calendars were generated. In Egypt the pattern of behaviour of the Nile dominated the seasons, and meteorological conditions at its sources, especially in the Ethiopian highlands, no doubt variable, affected its behaviour. Hence the approximate quarter day error in the 'vague' year as compared with the solar year would not show up readily in the short run, say a century or two, though in the long run it did. I shall discuss this point later. Most of the evidence points to the ancient Egyptians being a very conservative people and I shall rely somewhat on this view of them. There were now and then radical shifts in tradition, such as the shift to exclusive Sun-worship, but in general these shifts were short-lived.

I shall now turn to a brief discussion of the two luni-solar calendars, the earlier according to Parker preceding the civil calendar and the later being a schematic adjustment of the earlier one to the civil calendar. I shall state first what I find most convincing in Parker's account in these two luni-solar calendars and save till later those aspects of his account of the earlier one about which I have doubts.

Parker convinces me that the early luni-solar Egyptians calendar consisted of a year of usually 12 lunar months, measured from the day after the last visible crescent moon before sunrise and hence consisting of 29 or 30 days in rough alternation. He also convinces me that every second or third such years contained a thirteenth month of 29 or 30 days (depending on observation) and that this intercalary month was let in when the Sothic heliacal rising occurred so late in the month originally called *wp-rnpt* (meaning perhaps at first 'the opening of the year' and applied to the day of the Sothic heliacal rising as well as to the lunar month in which this day occurred) that the next year was in danger of beginning before the next Sothic heliacal rising. The intercalated month was called *Dhwtyt*, and a festival to Thoth was held in it. The normal first month of the year, *thy*, (later *Thoth*) was delayed one lunar month when *Dhwtyt* was introduced.

I should, perhaps, explain why I use such strange looking names as *wp-rnpt*, *Dhwtyt* and *thy*, where all the transliterations are consonants, including *y* in *thy* which has a value something like our *y* in 'yes' and not like our *y*'s in 'merry' or 'thy'. In ancient Egyptian writing, the consonantal skeleton of a word was provided and the reader was expected to supply the vowels, a convention found in other Hamitic and in many Semitic languages (see Gardiner, 1927).

I have difficulty in accepting Parker's view that in this early luni-solar calendar the rate of intercalation was nine times in 25 years, though I accept his evidence that this was the case with the later schematic luni-solar calendar based on calculation (rather than on observation) of the last visible crescent. This rate of intercalation seems to me to be quite appropriate for a schematic luni-solar calendar tied to a civil calendar with a 365-day year. Though the early Egyptians did not know that the average value of a lunar synodic month was about 29.5305879 days and the value of a tropical year (underlying the year of the seasons) was about 365.24249965 days *circa* 3000 BC, they would have had to live with the consequences in the long run of a few centuries of these periods. The discrepancy between 309 lunar synodic months and 25 tropical years (using the values just given) is about 6.1 days, which sums to about 24.4 days in a century. I do not believe that the early Egyptians could have lived with this degree of discrepancy if they were trying to get the lunar months right by observation and trying to get the year right. They may not have been trying to get the tropical year (e.g., from one Summer Solstice to the next) right. But on Parker's interpretation they were trying to keep the Sothic heliacal rising in the right lunar month. According to Schoch (1928) the period of Sothic heliacal risings at Memphis averaged 365.2507 days (though the period on particular occasions has to be 365 or 366 days). Again I do not expect the early Egyptians to have known Schoch's value but once again I assert that they would have had to have lived with the discrepancy of about 6.31584 days between 309 observed lunar months and 25 Sothic 'years', adding to about 25.26336 days in a century and 50.52672 days in two centuries of Sothic 'years'. With this rate of intercalation the Sothic heliacal rising could not have been kept in the month *wp-rnpt* for more than four cycles of 25 years. This rate of intercalation is, however, quite appropriate for approximate lunar months of 29 or 30 months with an intercalated month every two or, more usually, 3 years to keep them in near step with a 'vague' year of 365 days. Some 309 months of 29.5305879 days equal about 9124.95266 days and 25 years of 365 days equal 9,125 days, a discrepancy of only 0.04734 days.

I accept Parker's arguments about the later schematic Egyptian luni-solar calendar, instituted perhaps in the fourth century BC but possibly earlier. This calendar seems to have used a calculated first day of the month (related to the last visible crescent but slowly moving to a later day); as set out in the Carlsberg Papyrus it clearly used the rate of intercalation Parker wished to take back to the earlier luni-solar calendars and it almost certainly placed the intercalary months in the 25-year cycle so that its first day of the year never preceded the first day of the year of the civil calendar with its 365-day year. It would also follow that civil months and luni-solar months of the same name at least overlapped. I shall pay no further attention to this schematic luni-solar calendar other than to say that there are several instances of double-dating of some events in terms of both it and the civil calendar. These are useful in establishing both its pattern and in identifying particular years otherwise only approximately located.

Let me now turn to some further features of the civil calendar and to some problems concerning it.

Each civil month of 30 days was divided into three decades to mark the shift from one decans, the stellar 'hour hand', to the next for the marking of the hours of the night. They have been likened to the 7-day weeks and to the Roman 8-day *nundinum* but I am not aware that they were cycles of work ending in a day of rest, religious observance or marketing and other business. We have already learned that the day, reckoned from dawn to dawn, was divided into 24 unequal 'temporal hours' and that at least after a time, some form of sun-dial was used for measuring the sunlight hours and an ingenious water-clock used for an improved measurement of the night hours in the several seasons.

I shall now turn to some more contentious issues concerning the Egyptian civil calendar. When was it instituted? Why were 365 days selected? Remember that the sidereal year was about 365.25636 days, that the tropical year *circa* 3000 BC was about 365.24249965 days and the average interval between Sothic heliacal risings at Memphis was about 365.2507 days. How did the Egyptians who operated over such a long period come to overlook these discrepancies between their civil year and the solar years of approximately 0.25 days?

There is a great deal of evidence that the Egyptians from a quite early date regarded the Sothic heliacal rising as marking in some way the opening of the year. There is for instance a first dynasty tablet depicting a recumbent cow (Isis-Sothis) which has the sign for 'year' with a stroke between its horns and underneath a sign which may be read as a symbol for the season of Inundation. The hieroglyph for *wp-rnpt*, the opening or opener of the year is a pair of horns usually with the 'year' sign (like our letter *f* without the full cross stroke) between them or beside them. Parker (1950, p. 34) suggests that the tablet may be read 'Sothis' the opener of the year, the Inundation'. There are many later inscriptions, e.g., 'Ramses II rises like Isis-Sothis in the sky on the morning of *wp-rnpt*' or in the Canopus decree 'on the going forth of Sothis, called *wp-rnpt* (the opening of the year)'. These three span the whole dynastic period of Egyptian history.

I am convinced by Parker that earlier scholars created a problem for themselves in attaching the Sothic heliacal rising to the beginning of the civil calendar rather than to a marker relationship for the beginning of the earlier luni-solar calendar.

Assuming for the movement, as many commentators in the past did, that the intervals between Sothic heliacal risings were 365.25 days, it may be worked out (and I suspect that it was worked out in the mid-first millennium BC) that the day of the Sothic heliacal rising worked its way backwards through the Egyptian civil year at the rate of about 1 day in 4 years or 365 days in 1,460 years. The period of 1,460, reported by Censorinus in AD 238, is known as the Sothic Cycle. Let us see how it works. Suppose in some year x, the first day of *Thoth* is also the day of the Sothic heliacal rising. In the year $(x + 3)$, the second day of *Thoth* will be the day of the Sothic heliacal rising, and in the year (*x* + 119), the thirtieth day of *Thoth* will witness the going forth of Sothis. In this manner after 1,460 Sothic years or 1,461 Egyptian civil years from *x*, the Sothic heliacal rising will have worked its way back to the first day of *Thoth*.

The intervals between successive heliacal risings of a star on the Ecliptic will on average be the same as the sidereal year, namely 365.25636 days. As the interval on particular occasions must be expressed in whole days, most intervals will be 365 with about one in four being 366 days. As *Sothis, Sirius*, lies about 40° south in celestial latitude from the Ecliptic, the intervals between its heliacal risings are affected by: (i) the precession of the equinoxes; and (ii) the terrestrial latitude of the observer. Bickerman (1968) gives a table of schematic dates and times for Sothic heliacal risings at 200-year intervals from 500 BC to AD 300 and for observers at 46°N., 42°N., 38°N. and 34°N. in terrestrial latitude (and in effect the terrestrial longitude of Greenwich). The average interval for an observer at 46°N. may be found from this table to be 365.249112 days and for one at 34°N., 365.250475 days. By extrapolation (it has to be curvilinear from these data) a value of about 365.2508 days may be found for 30°N., a latitude slightly north of Memphis which seems to have been an Ancient Egyptian observation and reference point, much as Greenwich became later. Schoch (1928), a noted calculator of such matters, established that the average interval at Memphis between Sothic heliacal risings is 365.2507 days: I shall accept Schoch's value. Thus it follows that the day of the Sothic heliacal rising works its way back through a complete Egyptian civil year in 1,455.9 Sothic years or 1,456.9 Egyptian civil years and not 1,460 years as claimed by Censorinus.

Further, as 365.2507 days differs so little from the 365.25 days used in the Julian calendar, the day of the Sothic heliacal rising in about 3000 BC would have been about 17 July in the projected back Julian calendar and about 19 July on the eve of the Christian era.

Censorinus reported that the Sothic heliacal rising and the first day of *Thoth* coincided on 20 July (Julian calendar) in AD 139. The extant codices of Censorinus' work differ as to whether he wrote *ante diem XIII Kal. Aug.* or *ante diem XII Kal. Aug.*, that is either our 20 or 21 July (Julian). They agree that in the year in which he was writing, AD 238, the Egyptian new year began on what we call 25 June (Julian). As 25 leap years occurred in the Julian calendar between AD 139 and AD 238, the first day of *Thoth* would have moved forward from 20 July in AD 139 to 25 June in AD 238.

Believing that the Egyptian civil calendar must have been instituted when the first day of *Thoth* and a Sothic heliacal rising coincided, Meyer in 1904, as reported by Parker (1950) and Winlock (1940), went back from the coincidence reported by Censorinus to supposed earlier coincidences at 1,460-year intervals, namely 1321 BC, 2781 BC and 4241 BC. Further believing, on some archaeological evidence that the civil calendar was in operation before 2781 BC, he boldly declared that 17 July (Julian), 4241 BC was the first certain date in history. Though his argument may be impeccable there are grounds for questioning his premises. First, as we have seen the true Sothic cycle is not 1460 years but nearer to 1456 years. Second, on the basis of the table given by Bickerman and of Schoch's value, I calculate that the Sothic heliacal rising in the late fifth millennium BC would have occurred perhaps as early as 16 July (Julian). Third, more recent scholars produce evidence calling into question the view that late fifth millennium Egyptians could have produced the Egyptian civil calendar (see Neugebauer, 1942; and Parker, 1950). Fourth, there now seems to be little ground for believing that the Sothic heliacal rising and the beginning of the Egyptian civil year were ever tied. On the one hand a little calculation shows how quickly the two events got out of step with each other and on the other Parker produces convincing, if not conclusive, evidence that the Sothic heliacal rising, *wp.rnpt*, was used to govern the intercalation of an extra month in the old luni-solar calendar when that event occurred so late in its like-named month that in the next year it was likely to occur in the next month *thy*. It was unsafe to let the Sothic heliacal rising occur later than the eighteenth day of the month *wp-rnpt*. When it did occur later the next lunar month was regarded not as the regular *thy* following *wp-rnpt* but as the intercalary month *Dhwtyt*.

I have followed Parker and others in drawing attention to the fact that the Sothic heliacal rising occurred in the dynastic period of Egyptian history, say 3000 BC to about the eve of the Christian era on 17 to 19 July (Julian calendar projected back). In some ways this truth can be misleading. It seems to me more important to establish where it stood in the tropical year over this long period. In order to establish its position in the tropical year, I shall use the modern estimate of the tropical year in *circa* 1500 BC, midway through the Egyptian Dynastic period, and locate the Summer Solstice in the Julian calendar projected backwards. I shall thus use a tropical year of 365.24241055 days, as a good average value. Consulting Tuckerman's tables (1962), I find that in 'Memphis local time', the Summer Solstice of 45 BC occurred late on 24 June (Julian calendar) if that day be measured from midnight or about midway through it if it be measured from dawn as was the Egyptian convention. From that base it may be established that the Summer Solstice in 1500 BC occurred on 4 or 5 July (Julian) and in 3000 BC on or about 16 July, that is perhaps the day before the observation of the Sothic heliacal rising in 3000 BC.

The date of the Summer Solstice has more bearing on the rise of the Nile than has the Sothic heliacal rising, even though the latter may once have been a harbinger of the flood. The waters of the Nile come from two main sources. One is tropical East Africa where rain and melting snow feed the lake system which in turn feeds the White Nile. There is considerable evaporation from the lakes and from the swamps in the Sudan through which the White Nile passes. Nevertheless there is a fairly steady minor supply of water into the lower Nile from this source. The other source is in the Ethiopian highlands whence the results of heavy spring and summer rains heavily laden with silt come pouring down the Blue Nile and to a less extent the Atbara. It is the second source which generates the flood in the lower Nile and which provides the rich, reinvigorating deposit of mud on the arable land in the valley flats of Egypt. When the Ethiopian rains are heaviest the velocity of the lower river flow is greatest (the flood is both high and early) whereas when they are lightest the flood is sparse and late 'in the lower valley region. We have no records giving dates and heights of the flood in the dynastic period, though the records from the Cairo Nilometer from the seventh to the nineteenth century AD (see Popper, 1951) are informative in respect of what may have been the case earlier. The construction of dams both at the beginning of the White Nile and at Aswan high up the main Nile Valley in this century render recent records less valuable. From the records cited by Popper it is clear that there has been great variation in both the date of onset and in the magnitude of the flood and that over and above some evidence of cycles in these values there has been a progressive change from later to earlier floods and from more frequent to less frequent scanty floods. Part of these trends seem to be the result of the rise through silting of the height of the river bed, not to mention some variation over time in its banks. There could in addition be meteorological trends affecting rainfall in the Ethiopian highlands. Such considerations render dubious any extrapolation from largely second millennium AD records to the third millennium BC or earlier. Nevertheless, a drowning man is entitled to clutch at a straw.

The records Popper so exhaustively collated have direct information on the dates of the beginning of the rise of the Nile only in fairly recent times. There is indirect evidence, however, that it may often have occurred early in the second millennium AD in mid- to late June (Julian), that is, about the time of the Summer Solstice. During the present millennium, the rate of rise of the river at Cairo has at first been slight, then accelerates from late July through August and finally tapers off before the maximum height of the water is achieved usually in late September or early October. This reflects the pattern of rainfall and run-off in the Ethiopian highlands. The rains begin in early May, build up to a maximum in late July and then begin a decline in volume through August and September (see Popper, 1951 p. 256). Run-off into the feeder streams and flow into the lower Nile naturally lag behind the volume of rainfall.

For much of the present millennium and for almost half of the preceding millennium there is evidence, on other matters, for example, (i) the height of the river on 20 June (Julian), (ii) the date when 'plenitude' (16 cubits but differently assessed at different times) is reached, and (iii) the height of the river when it is at its maximum. From these data one can draw some rough inferences about the beginning of the flood. On these points I shall not go into the evidence in any detail, instead I shall concentrate on a few conclusions. First, from about the mid-seventh century AD (and we have no records earlier than that) the volume of the flood declined to a trough in the early ninth century; from the latter time it has progressively increased. I suspect that the increase has been in part a result of the build-up, through silting, of the river bed in the lower Nile, a process which must go back to the third millennium BC and earlier. This process cannot account for the earlier decline in the volume of the floods in the period examined by Popper. I suspect that decline to be the result of trends, possibly cyclical, in meteorological conditions in Ethiopia. Second, in the period for which dates of the 'plenitude' are available (eleventh to nineteenth centuries AD), the average date has moved forward in the year from about mid-September to early August (Gregorian). When in an earlier period (e.g., the seventh century), the volume of the flood was greater than it was in the eleventh century, I suspect the date of 'plenitude' was earlier than mid-September.

71

I am clutching at two straws. First, that the beginning of the flood advances because of the silting or build up of the river bed; second, that it oscillates because of cyclical meteorological conditions in the Ethiopian highlands (this being a very slender straw). I conclude that early in the third millennium BC on or about 16 or 17 July (Julian), the Summer Solstice occurred, Sirius (Sothis) made its heliacal rising and that the Nile at Memphis was usually about to begin its rise. Later I shall show how variable the last phenomenon may have been.

I shall now turn to an equally inconclusive consideration of what may have led the ancient Egyptians, possibly early in the third millennium BC (e.g. 3000 BC or a little after), to have picked on the 'vague' civil year of 365 days. We know, but they almost certainly did not, that it was about 0.24249965 days shorter than the tropical year in 3000 BC and about 0.2507 days shorter than the Sothic 'year'; further they seemed after a long time to have estimated that it was about 0.25 days shorter than one or other of these years. When Eudoxos, early fourth century BC, reported that the Egyptians had discovered the year to be 365.25 days, I suspect that the year in question was the Sothic 'year' and not either the tropical year or the sidereal year. If I am correct in this guess, this could have been the basis for Censorinus' estimate of the Sothic cycle as 1,460 years. Three hypotheses have been proposed concerning the origin of the 365-day Egyptian civil year, namely by Neugebauer (1942) but first proposed in 1938, by Winlock (1940) and by Parker (1950).

I find Winlock's hypothesis least convincing. He suggests that early in the third millennium BC the Egyptians had established that the intervals between Sothic heliacal risings were usually 365 days, sometimes 366 days (as a result of the excess of 0.2507 days over 365 days) and sometimes 364 days (as a result of poor viewing conditions on the occasion of the preceding observation) and consequently settled on 365 days, disregarding thereafter Sothic heliacal risings which subsequently got out of step with the 365-day cycle. One can readily enough imagine ancient people making imprecise observations and on their basis producing some neat schematization, but if the Sothic heliacal risings were so important for the Egyptians' determination of the length of the year, why did they ignore the mismatch of their civil year and the intervals between Sothic heliacal risings which would have so soon shown up, 1 day in 4 years, 10 days in 40 years and so on?

I accept Parker's view that 'the going forth of Sothis, the opening of the year, the inundation', a courageous interpretation of a simple

First Dynastic inscription, was not a reference to the Sothic heliacal rising marking the opening of the civil year of 365 days but to its use in deciding when to let in the intercalary month in the earlier luni-solar calendar.

Some more variable event than the Sothic heliacal rising must have been the basis of the 365 days as both Neugebauer and Parker argue. That is, some moderately variable recurring event which would not have been seen to be obviously wrong in the short run of 4, 40 or even 100 years.

Neugebauer (1938, 1942) selects the beginning of the flood, though both Winlock (1940) and Parker (1950) reject this as being too variable an event for its central tendency expressed in rounded days to be seen by the early Egyptians. Winlock cites modern records showing the intervals between the onset of the flood to be as short as 335 days or as long as 415 days. Both he and Parker argue that such variation would be scarcely likely to lead to an estimate of 365 days.

I have derived from the data provided by Popper on the dates of 'plenitude' when the river height reached 16 cubits, the intervals in days between successive 'plenitudes'. For some years there is either no record or an uncertain record, therefore, I am unable to give intervals for every year in the two periods which I have selected, namely AD 1382 to 1522 and AD 1693 to 1862. The date of 'plenitude' probably does not give an exact indication of the date of the beginning of the rise in water level. When the volume of the flood is great, the interval between the beginning of the rise and the attainment of 'plenitude' will be shorter than when the volume is slight. Nevertheless, intervals between 'plenitudes' should on average give a good indication of the intervals between the beginnings of the rise in successive years. Table 6.1 sets out frequency distributions of the intervals between 'plenitudes' for the two periods. The means for the two periods are 364.88 days and 365.29 days respectively. Though there are occasional very short intervals, for instance 338 days in the first period and 334 days in the second, and occasional very long intervals, for instance 396 days in the first period and 389 days in the second, as a result of an early flood following a late one or *vice versa*, most intervals cluster around 365 days, rather more tightly in the second period than in the first. This difference in the tightness of the clustering is probably a function of the floods being somewhat heavier in the second period than in the first, as attested by other data provided by Popper.

We do not know how the river was behaving in the early third

Intervals in days	Period	
	AD 1382–1522	AD 1693–1862
334–7	0	1
338–41	1	0
342–5	2	0
346–9	4	1
350–3	11	2
354–9	10	5
358–61	15	10
362–5	18	20
366–9	10	21
370–3	14	12
374–7	7	4
378–81	4	1
382–5	6	1
386–9	2	1
390–3	1	0
394–7	1	0
Total	104	79
Mean	364.88 days	365.27 days
355 to 375 d.	69 (66%)	71 (90%)
350 to 380 d.	87 (84%)	75 (95%)

Table 6.1   Frequency distributions of the intervals in whole days between 'plenitudes' in two periods. (Data based on Popper, 1951.)

millennium BC. It may be that the rise began a little later then than in the present millennium and that the floods reached lower maxima because of a less silted river bed, but it is unlikely that the pattern of intervals between the beginning of the rise (or between the attainment of some fixed height such as 'plenitude' or between the attainment of maximum height) was markedly different, provided of course that climatic conditions in the Ethiopian highlands were then not markedly more variable. Therefore, Winlock's and Parker's argument that the onset of the flood is too variable for the early Egyptians to have found the central tendency of the intervals, leaves me unconvinced. With so high a proportion of the intervals falling within 365 ± 10 days, I see no difficulty in the early Egyptians having noticed it and expressed it in whole days. I do not agree with Neugebauer that because they recorded the interval in whole days, the average must come out in whole days, but I do agree that the event was variable enough for them not to have worried for quite a long time (by then convention would be so strongly established as to relieve the worry) about any fractional departure of the real average from 365 whole days.

Parker's hypothesis is at first sight more plausible than Winlock's. Parker seems to me indubitably to have established the pattern of intercalation in the later schematic luni-solar Egyptian calendar. His evidence on this pattern is quite late. Nine embolistic years of 383, 384 (the most usual) or 385 days in 25 years otherwise usually 354 or 355 days certainly yields an average of about 365 days. I do not believe that Parker produces any evidence that this pattern obtained in the earlier true luni-solar Egyptian calendar in which the months were tied to the phases of the Moon. It is a poor pattern of intercalation for anyone who wants to observe the phases of the Moon and at the same time wishes to keep the schematic years on average in some modest run of time with the year of the seasons. This rate of intercalation leads to a discrepancy of about 6.1 days between 309 lunar synodic months and 25 tropical years or about 6.3 days between 309 lunar synodic months and 25 Sothic years. If Parker is correct, as I have accepted, in concluding that the intercalary month, *Dhwtyt*, was let in whenever there was a danger that in the next year the Sothic heliacal rising would occur after its month, *wp-rnpt*, had finished, then this rate of intercalation would ensure that just this delay would occur in the fifth cycle of 25 years. Therefore, I reject Parker's hypothesis about the origin of the 365 vague civil year.

The civil calendar remained unchanged in Egypt from its institution, it would seem, early in the third millennium BC until near the end of the first millennium BC. Ptolemy III Euergetes I in 238 BC issued a decree, now known as the Canopus decree from the site where an inscription proclaiming it was found in recent times, requiring that every fourth year have a sixth epagomenal day. The decree seems to have been ignored and it was only in 30 or 26 BC when Augustus issued a similar decree that the so-called Alexandrian calendar observing it began. Nevertheless, the old civil calendar with its regular 365 days lingered on. The Egyptian calendar referred to by Censorinus in AD 238 iş clearly the old one and not the newer Alexandrian calendar.

The calendar of the Coptic Christians in Egypt and in Ethiopia is the Alexandrian variant with month names changed from *Thoth* to *Tut*, from *Mesore* to *Misra*, and so on. Much earlier the Persians took the Egyptian civil calendar to their homeland at a time when as rulers of Babylonia they were encouraging the Chaldeans to improve the calendar indigenous to that region. But after a time they began reforms of the borrowed schematic Egyptian civil calendar to bring it into better step with the year of the seasons. Their first attempt in their homeland, perhaps on the Babylonian model, was to add a month when the schematic year got about a month ahead of the tropical year, that is in about every 123 or 124 years. Their second attempt adopted the model of Ptolemy III Euergetes I and of Augustus, namely to add a sixth epagomenal day about every fourth year. It was probably in pursuit of the rate of introducing the sixth epagomenal day that Omar Khayyam, mathematician, astronomer and poet, produced in the mid-eleventh century AD his remarkably accurate estimate of the tropical year; it was better than any other estimate produced until late in the nineteenth century. There has been a still later reform in this century which produced what is known as the National Iranian calendar. In ordinary years 1 month has 29 days, 5 have 30 days and 6 have 31 days, whereas in leap-years there are 6 months of 30 and 6 of 31 days. It is so arranged that the first day of the first month, *Farvardin*, begins usually on 21 March (Gregorian), the usual day of the Spring Equinox.

When the Parsees migrated from Persia to India they took with them what I suggest is the intermediate version of the Persian modification of the Egyptian civil calendar. Their 12 months each have 30 days, and there are 5 or 6 epagomenal days at the end of each year. However, in one version the first day of *Farvardin* is late in August (Gregorian) and in another it is late in July, perhaps a heritage of earlier divergence in Persia on the letting in of an intercalary month.

Though schematic rather than astronomically based the Egyptian civil calendar with its 365 days appealed through its very regularity to astronomers in what I shall call the middle period of the history of astronomy. Ptolemy in the second century AD used it as did Copernicus in the sixteenth century AD.

Though 17 July (Julian) 4241 BC is almost certainly not the first certain date in history, the calendar Meyer had in mind when he made this bold claim has almost certainly been the most durable. It seems to have existed without variation for about three millennia and then with slight variations among the Copts, Persians, and Parsees for up to another two millennia.

7/THE ROMAN CALENDAR

The Roman Calendar underwent a number of changes, major and minor, from perhaps as early as the seventh century BC up to the well-known Julian reform of it in 46 BC. Unlike the situation in Egypt where two or more calendars were simultaneously in operation for long periods, it seems that at any given time only one form of the Roman Calendar was in use. The Julian reform is well documented, though not as fully as I should like (see Samuel, 1972). Earlier changes and revisions are matters of great uncertainty because of inadequacies in the evidence. There are a few commentaries on the early calendars remaining to us but apart from that of Varro, who was mainly concerned with the etymology of festival names, month names and some other calendrical terms, they were written by persons who had never experienced the pre-Julian calendars in operation. Of greatest value are the commentaries of Varro (in *De lingua latina*, written in the mid-first century BC), of Plutarch (in his life of Numa, late first century or early second century AD), of Censorinus (in *De die natali*, early third century AD) and of Macrobius (in *Saturnalia*, *circa* AD 400). Each cites or quotes to greater or less extent earlier authors whose work does not remain to us and each makes clear that there was uncertainty about the calendar in its earliest form.

There are in addition various remarks, sometimes only in passing, in literary and historical writings on matters relating to the calendar. The fullest literary statement, namely Ovid's *Fasti*, has to do with the festivals and other special days which shall not concern us much. Some of these references, though some are textually suspect, are of great value as clues upon which to make certain judgements. For example, a reference by Cicero in *De re publica* to a report by Ennius that in some year about 400 BC an eclipse of the Sun occurred on the Nones of June indicates that by that date the month was no longer tied to the phases of the Moon as it is said by some commentators once to have been. The Nones of June is the fifth day of that month and would have been 6 or 7 days after the conjunction which is required for a solar eclipse and which would have preceded the first day of June were the month still tied to the lunar phases. Finally, there are some remaining inscriptions setting out the calendar, usually Julian but one fairly complete late pre-Julian (see Michels, 1967).

A common story is that Romulus, the alleged founder of the City of Rome, devised a calendar of 10 months, namely *Martius*, *Aprilis*, *Maius*, *Iunius*, *Quintilis*, *Sextilis*, *September*, *October*, *November* and *December*, (all these words are adjectival in form qualifying *mensis* usually left understood). It is claimed that *Martius*, *Maius*, *Quintilis and October* had 31 days and that the remaining 6 had 30 days. Both Censorinus and Macrobius say that the year of Romulus contained only 304 days but I suspect that this number is arrived at simply by addition of the number of days in each of the named months and that the year of Romulus, if it ever existed, had an unnamed couple of months in the dead of winter when not much was happening in agriculture (see Samuel, 1972, pp. 167 ff.).

The common story goes on to say that Numa Pompilius, the second King of Rome *circa* 700 BC added the two months *Ianuarius* and *Februarius* and brought the start of the year forward from *Martius* to *Ianuarius*. The name of the latter is said by many to derive from Janus, the god of gateways, who was usually represented with a face on the back as well as on the front of his head. Janus looked backwards as well as forwards, as the first month of the year may be thought to do. Censorinus and Macrobius say that Numa added 51 days to Romulus' year thus making the year 355 days and that he reduced the months which previously had 30 days to 29 days. With the added 51 days and the further 6 taken from *Aprilis*, *Iunius*, etc., he was able to give 29 days to *Ianuarius* and 28 to *Februarius*. They both claim that this distribution of the numbers was to maximize odd numbers which the Romans deemed to be lucky. Macrobius says that at first Numa added 50 days to Romulus' 304 to make the year 354 days and then added another to get a lucky number. Macrobius goes on to say that at some later time, he does not say when, an intercalary month was introduced into Numa's calendar late in *Februarius*. Plutarch says that Numa introduced this intercalation, though he does not agree with Macrobius about the number of days involved in it.

I am inclined to suggest that all of this was not very well informed backward speculation or rationalization. What was known by experience or by memory of the pre-Julian Republican calendar seems to have been taken back into an earlier period when there may have been a lunar or a luni-solar calendar with roughly alternating 29 and 30-day months based on observation of the first visible crescent. There are frequent references to the month having once been regulated by the Moon. For example, Varro says

> As the year is named from the motion of the sun, so the month is named from the motion of the moon until after departing from the sun she returns again to him (Kents' translation).

Macrobius claims that the Kalends was once fixed by observation of the first visible crescent and that the Ides originally was the day of the full Moon. Further it is interesting that Numa's year is said to have been of 355 days. Twelve lunar months, each on average about 29.53059 days, total about 354.36 days. Numa's year may therefore have been lunar, but if so there could be no months of 31 days (unless they were followed by a 28-day month). Of course if Numa's calendar were lunar, it would have quickly got out of step with the seasons unless it had an intercalary month, say three times in a cycle of 8 years as was provided for in the Greek *octaeteris*.

I shall now turn to the pre-Julian Republican calendar which Michels argues, from a careful gathering and scrutiny of available evidence, may have been instituted by the *decemviri*, *circa* 450 BC. It had the 12 named months also attributed to Numa's calendar and each had the number of days said by Macrobius and others to have been allotted by Numa. According to Michels (1967), every second year, but not necessarily so, February was shortened to 23 or 24 days and an intercalary month of 27 days let in before the beginning of March; its official name was *Intercalaris* though it seems also to have had the popular name *Mercedonius* as it brought additional wages for the year. There is a different account of the intercalation which I shall report later.

Before I deal with other matters I wish to set out more fully than in Chapter 1 how dates were indicated in both the pre-Julian and the Julian calendars. In each month, there were three marker or dividing days; *Kalendae*, the first day of the month, *Nonae*, the fifth day in the 'short' months in the pre-Julian calendar and the seventh day in the four pre-Julian 31-day months (*Martius*, *Maius*, *Quintilis* and *October*) and *Idus*, the thirteenth day, in the 'short' months and the fifteenth day in the four long months. *Kalendae* is said to come from the archaic verb *kalare*, to proclaim, as on it the *rex sacrorum* proclaimed the number of days to *Nonae* (when the people had to assemble in the city to hear when the month's festivals, court days and so on would occur); perhaps originally he proclaimed on it that it was the first day of the month and that the first quarter of the Moon would occur in so many days. As Michels points out any one outside the city who failed to receive the message given on *Kalendae* would be able to tell from the shape of the Moon when to go into the city if the assembly occurred on the day of the first quarter of the Moon. There can be no doubt about the origin of the word *Nonae*, namely ninth day, in the Roman inclusive system of counting, before *Idus*. Varro suggests as an alternative a derivation from *novus*, new (Moon), but the Nones can never have had anything to do with the new Moon. *Idus* is said by Varro to come from the Etruscan *Itus*, which Macrobius interprets as 'pledge of Jupiter' because the Moon is full. Macrobius suggests a possible alternative derivation from *vidus*, from *videndo* (seeing), again because of the full Moon. He favours a still further possibility, namely a derivation from the Etruscan verb *iduare*, to divide, again a hint that the full Moon divides the lunar month.

The Kalends of each month was dedicated to Juno and the Ides to Jupiter. Varro says, in a passage of dubious authenticity that on the Kalends, that the *rex sacrorum* announced the number of days to the Nones as follows '*Die te quinti calo, Iuno Covella*' or '*Septimi die te calo, Iuno Covella*'. It has been suggested that *covella* comes from *cavus*, hollow; in that case there is a reference to the thin crescent Moon. Why the *rex sacrorum* should announce 'I proclaim thee (or call thee forth), Iuno of the crescent Moon, on the fifth (or seventh) day', when in fact he was announcing when the Nones would be, puzzles me. Perhaps the custom whatever it was, was so long dead that Varro was confused about it. Macrobius later, and following another version of Varro's passage, says the priest called out '*Iuno Covella*' five times or seven times according to the interval to the Nones.

Nones to Ides constituted inclusively 9 days (8 in our reckoning) and Ides to the end of all months except *Februarius* and *Intercalaris* two such *nundinum* periods. As reported in an earlier chapter the Romans had another series of 'ninth' day periods running successively through the year and not in any co-ordination with dates in the months just as is the case with our weeks. The days in each such *nundinum* were marked on the displayed calendars by a letter A to H. In the painted calendars A was red and B to H black. The red letter day was the *nundinae*, ninth day, and a market day.

The day of a Kalends, Nones or Ides of a month was so simply labelled, for example, *Kalendae Ianuariae*, *Nonae Februariae* and *Idus Martiae*. The day before one of these marker days was usually labelled *pridie* followed, in the accusative case, by the name of the marker and of the month, thus *pridie Nonas Iunias* for what we call 4 June (the Nones being 5 June). For the second, third, fourth and so on days before the marker day, there were two methods of labelling, both involving inclusive counting. Thus what we call 3 June could be recorded either as *die tertio ante Nonas Iunias* (abbreviated to *III Non.Iun*) or as *ante tertium Nonas Iunias* (abbreviated to *a.d. III Non.Iun*) The Romans counted the days backwards until they came to the preceding marker day. Thus the last 16 days of 11 months, the last 15 of *Februarius* and the last 14 of *Intercalaris* were labelled *ante diem* (*x*, a number) *Kalendas* (qualified by the name of the next month). Thus our 25 March would be *a.d. VIII Kal. Apr.* This makes it easier to understand why commentators on the pre-Julian intercalation who had never experienced it claimed that 22 or 23 days were let in after 23rd February (or *a.d. VII Kal. Mart*) and that *Februarius* resumed at the end of the 22 or 23 days to complete its 'remaining' 5 days (see Michels, 1967).

Michels provides convincing evidence that *Intercalaris* was always 27 days and that it began either after 23 February (the festival *Terminalia* held in honour of Terminus, the god of boundaries, but later thought to commemorate the end of the year) or after 24 February (ordinarily the festival *Regifugium* which was delayed to the fifth, or in Roman counting the sixth, last day of *Intercalaris* when that month occurred).

If Numa in naming *Ianuarius* meant it to be the first month of the year, it has to be recognized that for many purposes the Romans persisted with *Martius* as the first day of the year and so keeping *Quintilis* to *December* as the fifth to twelfth months as their names proclaim.

Before I turn to the problem of how the intercalation was effected in the pre-Julian Republican calendar, I should like to say a little on the possible origins of the month names though there is great uncertainty about some of them. *Ianuarius* I have already dealt with, namely the month of the double-faced Janus, god of gateways and doorways. I should perhaps add a possible alternative, *ianua*, a doorway but as this word derives from or is the origin of *Ianus*, the alternative is scarcely different. Varro suggests that *Februarius* may come from *di inferi*, the gods of the lower world, because in that month expiatory sacrifices are made to them: this seems an implausible derivation. Varro himself perfers a derivation from *dies februatus*, purification day, a festival held on the fifteenth day of the month (the *Lupercalia*). *Martius* is clearly from Mars and was dedicated to the god of war. *Aprilis* has various origins offered for it. One offered by Macrobius and partly supported by Plutarch focuses on Venus, the goddess of love and so counteracting *Martius* which preceded it. It suggests the unlikely derivation of *Aprilis* (or a suggested earlier *Aphrilis*) from *Aphrodite*, the Greek name for Venus or, as an alternative a derivation, from *aphros* the Greek word for foam from which Aphrodite-Venus was supposed to have arisen. A second set of derivations relates to the verb *aperire*, to open, to uncover, to reveal. One of this set suggests that April, being the first full month after the Spring Equinox deemed to occur late in March, opens the year; I consider this to be unlikely, though some scholars favour it. Another in the set suggests that April is the month in which verdure begins to show forth or, as a variant, the month in which the air clears, that is, becomes less misty. A third depends on cognate words in other Indo-European languages. Kent (1958) in a footnote to his edition of Varro's *De lingua Latina* suggests that *Aprilis* may derive from an adjective *apero*—'second', not otherwise found in Latin, that is that *Aprilis* is the second month of the year. Varro suggests that *Maius* and *Iunius* come from *maiores*, elders, and *iuniores*, young men, respectively. Macrobius prefers a derivation of the former from Maia, the mother of Mercury, or from Maia, the Mother Earth (appropriate enough for the month of established spring) and of the latter from Juno under her Etruscan name. I find Macrobius more plausible than Varro, though both are speculative. *Quintilis* (sometimes *Quinctilis*), *Sextilis*, *September*, *October*, *November* and *December* present no problems as the names assert that they are the fifth, sixth, seventh, eighth, ninth and tenth months.

When Macrobius discusses intercalation in what he calls Numa's calendar (but which, following Michels, I am suggesting is the Republican calendar introduced by the *decemviri* in about 450 BC), he claims that at first it was carried out purely by rule and that only later did the pontifices expose it to their whims. He says that the rule was such that 22 or 23 intercalary days were let into every second year so that at the end of 2 quadrennia 90 days had been added and that in the next 2 quadrennia only 66 days were added; he does not say in what pattern, but one may surmise he had in mind 22 added days in every second year on three occasions but none in the fourth. He claims that this was a Roman adaptation of the Greek practice of the *octaeteris*, in which 3 years in 8 had a thirteenth month. I understand that Macrobius may have been an Egyptian, though a Roman citizen. I suggest that he misunderstood the Greek *octaeteris* which totalled about 2,923 days as against his 2,996 days for eight Roman years and that his alleged early Roman rule of intercalation was a sheer piece of rationalization.

Michels argues that from the establishment of the Roman Republican calendar, the ordinary years consisted of 355 days (slightly longer than 12 lunar months) and that every other year, if deemed necessary by the pontifices, an *Intercalaris* of 27 days was let in after a truncated *Februarius*, specifically after the twenty-third or twenty-fourth day of the latter month and so adding 22 or 23 days to the year (making it 377 or 378 days in length). The rate of intercalation of 45 days in 4 years ordinarily of 355 days would yield an average year of 366.25 days which in the long run would prove to be excessive. This could be corrected by leaving to some human authority the right to skip an intercalation usually after 22 years but occasionally after 24 years. I am not suggesting that the early Romans worked it out as precisely as this. I am only suggesting that they saw the need for such discretionary decision and that they left it to the pontifices, who through incompetence or political cunning, a matter for dispute (see Michels, 1967 and Samuel, 1972) abused the power given them.

I should like to examine two dates cited by Livy, to which my attention has been drawn by Michels, on which he reports eclipses to have occurred. They are, (i) *a.d. V Id. Quint* (11 July in our terms) in 190 BC, and (ii) *a.d. III Non.Sept.* (3 September) in 168 BC. According to Michels, though I have not checked her claim, modern calculations show that eclipses occurred in these years on 14 March and 21 June respectively in the Julian calendar projected back into the second century BC. Thus there is a shortfall in the pre-Julian dates given by Livy and the projected back Julian dates, quoted by Michels, of 119 days on the first occasion and 74 days on the second. It would seem that in the 22 year interval between the two eclipses two of the second-year intercalations had been omitted, and that prior to the first eclipse intercalations had been omitted at a greater rate than they were from the first to the second eclipse. All one can conclude is that the pontifices, for whatever reason, were failing to keep in reasonable step with the seasons the dates of festivals which had some seasonal significance. Julius Caesar, who as *Pontifex Maximus* was clearly for a long time recreant in this respect, later almost righted the whole convention.

There cannot be much doubt about what Julius Caesar did in what we now call 46 BC and about what he decreed for 45 BC and succeeding years. With the aid of Sosigenes, an Alexandrian Greek astronomer, Julius decreed that from our 45 BC onwards the years should average 365.25 days. He spread the near 10.25-day deficiency of the ordinary Republican Roman year of 355 days as follows: 2 extra days to *Ianuarius*, *Sextilis* and *December*; 1 extra day to *Aprilis*, *Iunius*, *September* and *November*; and 1 extra day to *Februarius* every fourth year. This gave a good, but as it proved in the not very long run a not good enough, approximation to the year of the seasons and to the tropical year, namely 365.24315 days.

Though there are differing reports as to what Julius decreed for what we call 46 BC, I have little doubt as to what he did. Censorinus, and Fotheringham (1931), a careful modern scholar, supports him, reports that Julius in 46 BC added after the twenty-fourth day of *Februarius* a standard *Intercalaris* with 27 days and that he added between *November* and *December* 2 unprecedented intercalary months adding together another 67 days. Not only was the latter intercalation after November quite unusual in this 'year of ultimate confusion', as it has been called, but also the choice of 67 days was unusual. It has sometimes been assumed that *Intercalaris* consisted of 22 or 23 days, though as Michels argues it seems always to have been of 27 days' duration. Sixty-seven days is not a sum of any pair of 22, 23, 27, 29 or 31 days. I take it, therefore, that the 67 days (or the 23 plus 67 days) were chosen by Julius on Sosigenes' advice to get the dates back into step with some earlier convention. I am puzzled as to what it may have been. Julius was in many ways a conservative reformer. He left the earlier *Martius*, *Maius*, *Quintilis* and *October* with their 31 days, the ordinary *Februarius* to its 28 days and he inserted the extra day in that month in leap years where the earlier *Intercalaris* had often begun, namely after the twenty-fourth day, *ante diem sextum Kalendas Martias* (Julius' intercalated day was called *ante diem bis sextum Kalendas Martias*, the second 'sixth' day before the March Kalends). It is true that he added a day or two to the other months, making some of them an unlucky 30 days in length. But what was he seeking in adding 90 days in 46 BC? Several suggestions have been made, none of which I find convincing.

During the early part of the first millennium AD it seems to have been assumed that the equinoxes and solstices in the Julian calendar did or should occur on 25 March, 24 June, 24 September and 25

	Average intervals in days between	
Season	Equinoxes and Solstices	24th or 25th day of specified months (Julian)
Spring	92.76	91
Summer	93.66	92
Autumn	89.84	92
Winter	88.98	90.25
Total	365.24	365.25

Table 7.1   Comparison of the intervals in days between (i) equinoxes and solstices, and (ii) 25 March, 24 June, 24 September and 25 December in the Julian calendar. Spring means Spring Equinox to Summer Solstice in the first case or 25 March to 24 June in the second, and so on. In Winter allowance is made for leap year.

December. According to Newton (1972), Pliny the Elder writing *circa* AD 77 claimed that the traditional Roman dates for these events were the seventh day (eight in Roman reckoning) before the Kalends of April, July, October and January, that is 25 March, 24 June, 24 September and 25 December. The days of conception and birth of John the Baptist and of Jesus were set to these dates as I have reported above. The intervals between the equinoxes and solstices expressed in whole days do not match the intervals between the dates in the 4 months just specified (see Table 7.1) though it would not have been difficult to make the duration of the schematic months such as to ensure a nearer match. Further, it is clear that if Julius were trying to get the Spring Equinox on 25 March in 45 BC, he failed, but if ne were aiming at the Summer Solstice on 24 June, he succeeded. According to my interpolations in Tuckerman's tables (1962), these events occurred at about 0.15 a.m. on 23 March and at about 11.46 p.m. on 24 June respectively in that year. Until the reigns of the Sun-worshipping emperors Elagabalus (AD 218–222) and Aurelian (AD 270–275) when 25 December was chosen as *Dies Natalis Solis Invicti* apparently in the mistaken belief that that was the date of the Winter Solstice, the only Roman festival which seems to have been associated with an equinox or solstice was *Fors Fortuna* on 24 June (see W. Warde Fowler, 1899). Possibly Julius was aiming to get its accepted date right in the year of the seasons. Richmond (1956), without citing any evidence for his claims, says that Julius would have liked to set his first *Kalendae Ianuariae* to the Winter Solstice but instead set it some days later in order to have it coincide with a new Moon, which Richmond says was important to the Romans. Warde Fowler also claims that a new Moon occurred on 1 January 45 BC. The Romans some centuries before may have been starting their months on the day of the first visible crescent but this was only a memory in the knowledge of learned men like Varro in Julius' lifetime. Consulting Tuckerman's tables, I find by interpolation that a lunar-solar conjunction occurred a little before midnight in Rome on 1 January 45 BC (Julian). The sun set in Rome about 4.40 p.m. ('local Roman time' calculated from data in *Norton's Star Atlas and Reference Book* (1957), the next day, that is about 17 hours 30 minutes after the conjunction. It is therefore most unlikely that a first crescent could have appeared in Rome before 3 January.

There are many examples of conservatism in Julius' reform of the Republican calendar. He left the intervals between Kalends and Nones, and between Nones and Ides undisturbed in each month. He inserted his intercalary day in February at one of the two points where the former month *Intercalaris* began. He left an ordinary *Februarius* with 28 days and *Martius*, *Maius*, *Quintilis* and *October* with 31 days. However, in spreading the added 10 days in ones or twos among the remaining months he disturbed the double *nundinum* period between the Ides of these months and the Kalends of their successors—something, of course, had to give. All this suggests to me that in adding just 67 days in his two unusual intercalated months in 46 BC he had some conservative aim in mind, but what it was escapes me, unless it was related to *Fors Fortuna*.

I have already told the story of Pope Gregory's reform of the Julian calendar in AD 1582, so this might be deemed to be an appropriate point to end. However, when one falls into a trap set by former writers and then escapes from it, it seems desirable to warn other readers about it. For some time I accepted the following story: Julius gave *Februarius* 29 days in ordinary years and 30 in leap years, *Sextilis* (our August) 30, *September* 31, *October* 30, *November* 31 and *December* 31. After his assassination the Senate in gratitude of his services changed the name of *Quintilis* to *Julius* in his honour. Later Augustus decreed that *Sextilis* should be re-named *Augustus* in his honour and so that it should not be a day shorter than Julius' month he robbed *Februarius* of a day and then transposed the 30 to 31-day alteration of the months *September* to *December*. This fiction seems to have been enshrined in an article on Calendars in late nineteenth-century editions of *The Encyclopaedia Britannica*, though I have seen it claimed that the error goes back at least to John of Holywood (Sacrobosco), the thirteenth-century author of *The Treatise on the Spheres* mentioned by Chaucer in his *Treatise on the Astrolabe* (late fourteenth century). Though Augustus may have inspired the change of name of the old *Sextilis*, the formal change seems to have been carried out by a vote of the Senate just as the earlier change of *Quintilis* had been effected. All the rest of the story is false. Augustus did, it seems, intervene in about 8 BC in the application of Julius' rule for the designation of a leap year. When Julius decreed that the leap year with the extra day in *Februarius* should occur every fourth year, his Egyptian Greek adviser, Sosigenes, may have overlooked the Roman custom of inclusive counting. At any rate the pontifices, after Julius' death, added the extra leap year day in every third year. Augustus declared a moratorium of leap years from about 5 BC until AD 8 in order to correct the error (see Samuel, 1972).

8/THE BABYLONIAN CALENDARS

The Babylonian calendars, or more precisely the ancient Mesopotamian calendars of Sumer, Babylon and Assyria, as well as their Jewish and Greek derivatives or parallels, were luni-solar. That is, they attempted to get the lunar month right at least to the rounded day and to get the year of the seasons roughly right on average. The Mesopotamian calendars underwent so little basic change that it is tempting to speak of them in the singular.

The Mesopotamian calendar almost certainly began among the Sumerians who had settled in the lower Euphrates valley perhaps in the fourth millennium BC or even earlier. It was later adopted by the South Akkadians in Babylonia and passed on by them to the North Akkadians in Assyria. It was adopted by the Jews, and it probably influenced Greek calendrical practices. It survived the Persian, the Greek and the Parthian conquests of Mesopotamia but not the Mohammedan conversion.

When it began it may have been a purely lunar calendar with the months starting on the evening of the first visible crescent Moon. Granted favourable viewing conditions this would yield, as we have seen in Chapters 2 and 4, months of 29 and 30 days in rough alternation. The day was deemed to begin at sunset; so the first day of the month, either the day of the first visible crescent or the thirtyfirst day since the last first visible crescent, was usually marked by a thin crescent in the western sky at its very beginning.

The Sumerians were an agrarian people with a well organized system of city-state government—making laws, collecting taxes, providing services, etc. Hence the year of the seasons would be important for them. After a time it would have become apparent to them that every now and then a thirteenth month had to be added to the twelve which they had taken to be a year. There appears to have been some uncertainty about the length of the year of the seasons. It has been suggested that quite early the Sumerians took it to be 360 days, about 5 or 6 days longer than 12 months of 29 or 30 days and 5 or 6 days shorter than the tropical year. This is plausible. The Sumerians had a sexagesimal number system, hence the year may have been deemed properly to be some multiple of 60. Either they or their successors, the Babylonians, divided the circle into 360°, a division believed by some to have been based on the Sun's eastward progression among the fixed stars at about 1° per day. However, an estimate of the year as 360 days would have been found in the course of time to be wrong, as would the better estimate of 365 days. On what basis the Sumerians decided to let in an extra or thirteenth month we do not know. Perhaps Hammurabi in Babylon in the early second millennium BC was following a Sumerian practice when he issued the decree mentioned in Chapter 4; the year was obviously ending too soon as seen by the state of the crops or other agrarian events, so an extra month was let in.

The Sumerians named the months in accordance with a series of adventures by mythical nature heroes, events clearly of a seasonal kind. The south Akkadians of Babylonia translated these names into their own language though they do not seem to have taken over the myths. Thus we have the Babylonian months as follows:

1. *Nisanu*	7. *Tashritu*
2. *Airu*	8. *Arasamnu*
3. *Simanu*	9. *Kislinu*
4. *Duzu*	10. *Tebetu*
5. *Abu*	11. *Shabatu*
6. *Ululu*	12. *Addaru*

In the Babylonian scheme, *Nisanu* ordinarily began at about the time of the Spring Equinox, *Duzu* at about the Summer Solstice, *Tashritu* at about the Autumn Equinox and *Tebetu* at about the Winter Solstice, or were meant so to begin. When there was an apparent deficiency in the year or half-year which was about to end, the extra or intercalary month was let in. Early practice, as evidenced in Hammurabi's decree added a second *Ululu* which suggests that the year may have been deemed to begin with *Tashritu*, that is about the time of the Autumn Equinox. Later practice favoured a second *Addaru*, which points to the year beginning at the Spring Equinox. There is other evidence which suggests that quite early the year was deemed to begin with a first visible crescent on or around the Spring Equinox. For instance, the zodiacal constellation which we still call *Taurus* was sometimes referred to as the Bull-in-Front (see Payne-Gaposchkin, 1954). About 3000 BC the Sun was making his Spring crossing of the celestial Equator while about midway in the constellation of *Taurus*.

It has been suggested that the Babylonians perhaps in the early part of the first millennium BC introduced a rule of intercalation like that used by some Greek city-states in the middle of that millennium. The evidence for this may not be conclusive, but I shall at this point explain more fully the Greek practice, the *octaeteris*, to which I have already referred in Chapters 4 and 7. In a cycle of 8 years, 5 years had 12 months and 3 had 13 months. Thus 99 lunar months were equated with 8 solar years. Let me check this equation using modern estimates for the lunar synodic month (29.5305879 days) and for the tropical year *circa* 750 (365.2423615 days). Ninety-nine such synodic months total 2923.528202 days, whereas eight such tropical years total 2921.93892 days, a difference of about 1.589 days. In one sense this check is not fair to the Greeks or to the Babylonians for they did not have the values I have used. Nevertheless they would have had to have lived with the discrepancy of about 1.6 days per 8 years even though it may have taken them several *octaeteris* cycles to have discovered any noticeable discrepancy. It may seem fairer to use the values established by Naburimannu, the Babylonian, in about 500 BC. Eight of his years of 365.2609 days total 2922.0872 days and 99 of his months of 29.530614 days total 2923.530785 days, leaving a discrepancy of about 1.44 days. His values may have been based on this discrepancy.

In 432 BC Meton, a Greek astronomer, enunciated a better rule of intercalation than the *octaeteris*; it has long been known as the Metonic Cycle. It consisted of a cycle of 19 years, 7 of which were embolistic, that is, having a thirteenth or intercalary month. Thus he equated 235 lunar months of 29 or 30 days with 19 years. Nineteen years of 365.24234615 days (the tropical year *circa* 500 BC) total about 6939.605 days, whereas 235 lunar months averaging 29.5305879 days total about 6939.688 days, a discrepancy of only about 0.083 days or just less than 2 hours. Meton rounded the 235 lunar months and the 19 solar years to 6940 days. Later Kallippos (fourth century BC) and Hipparchos (second century BC) suggested improvements of the Metonic Cycle, through the introduction of some cycles of only 6939 days. Though Greek astronomers used the Metonic Cycle for their purposes, no Greek city-state seems with certainty to have adopted it for civil purposes (see Samuel, 1972 pp. 52 ff.).

There are indications (see Parker and Dubberstein, 1956) that the Babylonians were groping for something like the Metonic Cycle from as early as the late seventh and early sixth century BC when Nabopolassar (625–605 BC), the first Chaldean king and his son Nebuchadnezzar (605–562 BC) occupied the Babylonian throne and that they had almost got it by the time of Nabunaid (556–539 BC) who was the last Chaldean king, apart from two short-lived revolts in 522 and 521 BC against Persian rule. The Persian dynasty in Babylonia began in 539 BC and survived until about 331 BC when Alexander conquered the area. Though the Persians took the Egyptian civil calendar into their homeland, they preserved and improved, with the aid of the Chaldean priests, the Babylonian calendar in Mesopotamia.

Though there is some speculation and much calculation underlying the table of years with intercalated months provided by Parker and Dubberstein (1956) from say 633 BC, the general pattern for which they argue seems well enough supported by recorded evidence. Without further question, I shall accept their reconstruction. I reproduce one of their tables exhibiting this reconstruction.

Year in cycle	_ Cycle beginning in year BC _															
	633	614	595	576	557	538	519	500	481	462	443	424	405	386	367	348
1		A			A		U	A								
2			A			U								A		
3				U	A	A	A	A	a	A	A	A	A		A	A
4		U														
5	U		A	A	A											
6						A	A	A	a	a	a	A	A	A	A	A
7																
8	U	A	A	A					a	A	A	A	A	A	A	A
9		A				U	U									
10	A															
11							A	A	A	A	A	A	A	A	A	A
12		U	U		U	U										
13	U			U												
14			A	A	A	A	A	A	A	A	A	A	a	A	A	A
15	A	U														
16																
17			U	A	A	A	A	U	U	U	A	A	U	U	U	U
18	U															
19		U	A					A	A	A	A	A	A	A	A	A

Table 8.1 Intercalated months in 19-year cycles from 633 to 330 BC. A is for *Addaru* and U for *Ululu* where there is certain recorded evidence; a is for *Addaru* where there is only probability. (Adapted from Parker and Dubberstein, 1956.)

91

Several features of the data in this table call for comments. First, in the first eight 19-year cycles, beginning in 633 BC, there are four cases of 7 intercalated months, two cases of 8, one of 6 and one of 5, almost averaging 7 per cycle. Second, in the second eight 19-year cycles, beginning in 481 BC, there are in every case 7 intercalated months. Third, from quite early, there is a tendency to intercalate in the third, the sixth, the eighth, the eleventh, the fourteenth, the seventeenth and the nineteenth years in the cycle; this becomes standard, with one exception, after 481 BC. Fourth, though a second *Ululu* is frequent in the earlier cycles, a second *Addaru* becomes almost standard except in the seventeenth year from about 500 BC. Fifth, it may be added, that from 367 BC, the pattern there revealed prevailed until the demise of the Babylonian calendar when it was replaced in the Middle East by the Mohammedan calendar. The final standardization of the Babylonian calendar occurred in the reign of the Persian Artaxerxes II (405–350 BC).

By the time of the adoption of a cycle of 19 years with 7 of them having an intercalated month, the Chaldean priest-astronomers were probably calculating in advance the likely dates of the first visible crescent and perhaps more approximately the dates of turning points (e.g., the Spring Equinox) in the year. The values provided by Naburi-mannu and improved by Kidinnu would have enabled this, though occasional checking of predictions through observations would have been necessary to prevent serious cumulative discrepancies. The early preference for a second *Ululu* may suggest that the year was deemed to begin about the time of the Autumn Equinox; however, it is more likely that autumnal agrarian events such as the state of the crops and the fruiting of the vines, were clearer markers of the state of the beginning of the second half of the year. With a resort to calculation greater attention seems to have focused on 1 *Nisanu*. From some data given by Parker and Dubberstein, partly early records and partly reconstruction, it seems that in the late seventh century BC 1 *Nisanu* did not occur earlier than 6 March (Gregorian) or later than 13 April—a 38-day range. In the late sixth century the range was down to 28 days, 22 March to 20 April. In the early fourth century it was 29 days, 25 March (allowing a safety margin of a few days after the Spring Equinox) to 21 April, and it remained thus for the rest of the history of the Babylonian calendar. The Chaldeans may not have been able to establish the occurrence of the Spring Equinox by observation with a precision of less than a day or two. They seem not to have been as concerned as were the slightly later Greeks with establishing the dates of the equinoxes and solstices with precision (see van der Waerden, 1953). It does seem that they may have wanted to start the year with a first day of *Nisanu* just after the Spring Equinox. Any date later than about 21 April (Gregorian) for 1 *Nisanu* could be the day of the following first visible crescent and they were obviously not taking any risks by using a date earlier than 25 March (Gregorian) as the earliest for 1 *Nisanu*. It can be readily enough shown that to achieve these objectives together with the matching of 235 months and 19 years, they had little alternative to having the years with the intercalary month fall in the positions they in fact occupied in the cycle.

Sachs (1952b) suggests a slightly different basis for the years chosen in the 19 years as embolistic years and for the choice of a second *Ululu* on one occasion and a second *Addaru* on all the others. From a study of some records of the heliacal rising of Sirius, dating from the Seleucid Era, he claims that the intercalations by year and by month were so arranged that the Sirius heliacal rising was confined to the one lunar month, *Duzu*, whereas Spring Equinoxes were allowed to shift from the middle of *Addaru* to the middle of the second *Addaru* and the Summer Solstice from the middle of *Simanu* to early in *Duzu*. Granted that Sachs is correct in his inferences, the Babylonians in this period, and perhaps earlier, were using a rule of intercalation similar in principle to that argued for by Parker in the case of the earlier Egyptian luni-solar calendar. We shall see later the rather different rules for intercalation used by the Hindus and by the Chinese who also employed the Metonic Cycle.

The Chaldean calendar perfected under the Persian Achaemenid dynasty was preserved under the Hellenistic Seleucid dynasty with a change of names of the months to those used in Macedonia, for example *Nisanu* to *Artemisos*, and under the Parthian Arsacid dynasty. Under the latter it continued into the Christian era. It is preserved in modern form in the present-day Jewish calendar. I shall draw attention to some similarities and differences in the two.

First, the modern Jewish ordinary year consists of 12 months most with a fixed number of days as follows:

1. *Tishri* (30 days)
2. *Cheshvan* (29 or 30 days)
3. *Kislev* (30 or 29)
4. *Tebeth* (29)
5. *Shebat* (30)
6. *Adar* (29 or 30)
7. *Nisan* (30)
8. *Iyyar* (29)
9. *Sivan* (30)
10. *Tammuz* (29)
11. *Ab* (30)
12. *Elul* (29)

All these names derive from the Akkadian names. However, whereas *Nisanu* was the first month of the Babylonian year, *Tishri* replaces it in that role in the Jewish religious calendar. The months alternate in an approximate way between 29 and 30 days, but on a fairly fixed pattern which has little to do with the actual lunar synodic months, though the general scheme fits them moderately well.

Second, in 7 years, the same ones as used by the Chaldeans, in a cycle of 19, there is an intercalary month. The intercalary month is always a second *Adar*. In an ordinary year *Adar* has 29 days whereas in a 'long' year *Adar* has 30 and the second *Adar* 29 days. The variability of *Cheshvan* and *Kislev* arises from the wish to avoid the coincidence of the New Year's Day and a Sabbath. This may be done by adding a day to the *Cheshvan* (ordinarily 29 days) in the year before such a foreseen clash and taking it away from *Kislev* (ordinarily 30) in the following year or by taking it from *Kislev* before the clash and adding it to *Cheshvan* in the following year. One of the alternatives is sometimes preferable to the other because it eases other festival problems. The result of this manoeuvre is that some 'short' years have only 353 days, a feature of no other luni-solar calendar about which I have read.

The Jewish calendar was not always as I have just described it. The Jews may originally have had a luni-solar calendar with intercalations made on an *ad hoc* basis. They seem to have adopted the emerging Chaldean calendar during the Babylonian exile, though there is evidence that they were still relying on observations of first visible crescents when the Babylonians were relying more on calculation. Though there are many references to dates, for example the xth day of the yth month, in the Old Testament and many references to periods of days, months and years, there is virtually no general calendrical information and great subtlety is required to construct something simple and consistent from these references. However, in some apochryphal books, for example, *Enoch* and *The Book of Jubilees*, and in some parallel Dead Sea Scrolls (see Beckwith, 1970) there is a good deal of information and some fulmination against those who measure time by the Moon, but I shall not at this point go any further into this interesting material. Early in the Christian era the Jews began standardizing the calendar they had borrowed, using for some purposes Kidinnu's values for the month and for the year. I understand that the present form of the Jewish calendar was finally established early in the present millennium.

Though I feel confident that the Jewish calendar at least from the

Babylonian exile was basically Babylonian in the general sense in which I have been using the term, I am not so confident about the many Greek calendars which had many similar features to those to be found in the Babylonian calendar. One problem arises from the lack of sufficiently detailed information about the early Greek calendars and another from their great diversity in at least minor ways (see Samuel, 1972, Chapter 3). The calendars of the many city-states used different month names, a variation which probably arose from different stressed festivals and different emphasis on the members of the pantheon and different starting points for the year (see Table 8.2). Analogous months, however named, did not begin on the same days because it would seem scrupulous Moon-watching was neglected or difficult to conduct in Greek terrain and climate. Fixing the months by some sort of rule rather than by careful observation seems to have been common. Nevertheless, the months were kept tied, at least approximately, to the phases of the Moon and every now and then an intercalary month was let into the year. The Macedonians are said to have had an intercalary month every other year, a rate of intercalation that is, as we have seen, quite excessive. Many others used the *octaeteris* which has already been described. Meton has his name attached to the 19-year cycle described above but, as stated above, no civil Greek calendar seems to have used it, though Greek astronomers did.

The Greek calendar which has been most thoroughly investigated is that of Athens, but even in respect of it such experts as Meritt (1961) and Pritchett (1963) seem to be in disagreement on some matters of detailed interpretation of the fragmentary evidence. Though I shall forbear from entering the debate, I shall, however, mention one feature of Athenian dating, namely the day within the month and also the day within the period during which one of the several prytanies was in control. Originally there were ten tribal groups whose fifty representatives on the Council of Five Hundred took it in turn to act as a standing committee for the Council for some 36 or 37 days. The name of the prytany and the ordinal day of its representatives' period of control was used as a second date supplementing the lunar month name and the ordinal day within that month (see Meritt). Such double dating as I have already remarked is often helpful to the chronographer in identifying a particular year when it is uncertain which year in some short run is being referred to. Rather late in Athens the number of prytanies was increased, but provided that one knows the number of prytanies at a given epoch, the double dating is still useful.

ATHENS	AETOLIA
Hekatombaion*	Laphraios
Metageitnion	Panamos
Boedromion	Prokoklios*
Pyanepsion	Athanaios
Maimakterion	Boukatios
Poseideon**	Dios**
Gamelion	Eusaios
Anthesterion	Homoloios
Elaphebolion	Hermaios
Mounychion	Dionysios
Thargelion	Agyieos
Skirophorion	Hippodromios

BOEOTIA	MACEDONIA
Hippodromios	Loios
Panamos	Gorpaios
Pamboiotios	Hyperberetaios
Damatrios	Dios*
Alalkomenios**	Apellaios
Boukatios*	Audnaios
Hermaios	Peritios
Prostaterios	Dystros
Agrionios	Xandikox
Thiouios	Artemisios
Homoloios	Daisios
Theilouthios	Panemos

Table 8.2   Month names in four Greek city-states. The first month in each list correspond at least approximately to one another. The first month of the year is marked by a single asterisk; the month marked with a double asterisk is the one usually duplicated in an embolistic year. (Month names transliterated from a table in Bickerman, 1968.)

I have already mentioned that the Athenians in the classical period divided the month of 29 or 30 days into rough thirds. The first 10 days and the second 10 days were counted forwards, whereas the last 9 or 10 days of the month were counted backwards. This practice of counting the days backwards from the end of the month suggests that the number of days in the month were determined by calculation and did not await observation of the first visible crescent as in Babylonia. It also provides the only analogue I have encountered to the Roman custom of counting the days back from the Kalends, the Nones and the Ides. The threefold division of the Athenian month into 10, 10 and 10 or 9 days resembles the division of the Egyptian civil month of 30 days into three decades.

I presume that analogous practices may have been adopted in other Greek calendars, though we lack clear evidence. It would seem that most Greek calendars followed at least roughly the phases of the Moon to define the months, that they all had occasional intercalated months let in perhaps according to different rules, amongst which the *octaeter-'s* came to be favoured). They had varying conceptions of the beginning of the year, the first visible crescent on or after the Spring Equinox or the Summer Solstice or the Autumn Equinox, sometimes wrongly assessed. Just as the Roman pontifices played ducks and drakes with intercalation, the several Greek city-state authorities seem, perhaps within narrower limits, to have done likewise. Meton seems to have anticipated the Babylonians' introduction of the 19-year cycle with 7 embolistic years, though they seem to have thought of it in approximate form before him. Apart from the division of the months into decades, I suggest but cannot prove that the basic Greek schemes of months and years were borrowings from Babylonia. As they are based on readily enough observable astronomical periods, they could, of course, have been independent inventions.

9/INDIAN CALENDARS

Perhaps the most complex history of calendrical practices and the most complex set of practices in any one region is to be found in the Indian sub-continent. The ancient Egyptians, as we have seen, had in succession and for overlapping periods at least three basic calendars: first, a luni-solar calendar (possibly based on a still earlier lunar calendar); second, a civil calendar with a 'vague' year of 365 days (divided into 12 schematic months of 30 days plus 5 epagomenal days); and last, a schematic luni-solar calendar tied to the civil calendar. Though the Romans had a succession of calendars, each seems to have arisen by reform of an earlier version and to have had undisputed succession. The Babylonian calendars underwent similar evolutionary change though on different lines, as did the Hebrew calendar from at least post-Exilic times. Among the Greek city-states we found some marked local variations of what was a basic general scheme. Similar regional variations are to be found in India. In addition, however, are religious sect differences based on quite different schemes from that generally prevailing: one need only mention the Mohammedans with their lunar calendar and the Parsees with their two versions of what was the Egyptian civil calendar modified in Persia.

In late Vedic times, the Hindus had a somewhat crude schematic luni-solar calendar which they later sought to improve. The improvements came partly from importations including local innovations based on imported conceptions. The importations seem to have come from Babylonia, but probably through a Hellenistic Greek medium. In the long run three calendars in simultaneous operation were generated: one a solar civil calendar with schematic months of 30 or 31 days; the second a solar calendar with 'solar months' marked off by the Sun's entry into successive signs of the Zodiac; and the third a luni-solar calendar with the months measured from new Moon to new Moon or in some regions from full Moon to full Moon and with the intercalation of the thirteenth month governed by one of the solar calendars.

In the late Vedic period, say the second half of the first millennium BC, though the practice may have had a much earlier origin (see Renou and Filliozat, 1953), ordinary years consisted of 12 months of 30 days (which therefore would get out of step with the lunar months marked by the phases of the Moon). The months were grouped in pairs to constitute five seasons, the names of which, *vasanta, grishma, varsha, sarad, hemanta* and *sisira*, may be loosely translated as 'spring', 'summer', 'rains', 'autumn', 'winter' and 'frosts' (or 'mists'). Every 5 years, a period which was called a *yuga* (yoke), a thirteenth month was added to the year. In the earliest extant accounts this intercalary month was also one of 30 days, thus making the *yuga* a period of 1830 days, whereas *circa* 500 BC 5 tropical years totalled about 1826.8 days. Apparently to reduce this discrepancy of about 3.2 days in 5 years, a later practice made the intercalary month 25 or 26 days, which made the average calendar year, between 365 and 365.2 days, slightly shorter than the year of the seasons. One is tempted to notice two analogies, first the use of 30-day schematic months like those of the Egyptian civil calendar and second the later use of a shortened intercalary month akin in some ways to the shortened Roman *Intercalaris*. I suggest that both analogies are better regarded as coincidences rather than as evidence of influence.

A Vedic convention which has survived in modern Indian calendrical practice involves the 27, or sometimes 28, *nakshatra* segments, already introduced in Chapter 5. These, as we have learned, were originally named stars or star groups which the moon in its 27.32 day circumnavigation of the heavens caught up with night by night. Thus, if early in one night the Moon was level, in longitude, with the Pleiades (*Krittika* in Sanskrit), then at about the same time on the next night the Moon would be level with *epsilon Tauri*, (*Rohini* in Sanskrit), one of the Hyades, and on the third night with *lambda Orionis* (*Mrigasiras*). The 27 stars differ in celestial longitude by about 13° (plus or minus several degrees). On the twenty-eighth night, the Moon catches up again with *Krittika*, though at a rather earlier hour than on the initial occasion; this may be deduced from the fact that the Moon's average sidereal period is 27.32 days and not a round 27 or 28 days. It was this slight mismatch which seems to have led in some lists to a twenty-eight *nakshatra* star, called *Abhijit* (Vega, *alpha Lyrae*) only a few degrees in longitude beyond its predecessor *Uttarvasadhah* (*sigma Sagittarii*). This marking off by means of designated stars of the Moon's progress night by night around the heavens is as we have seen similar in principle to the Egyptian use of a series of stars (the decans) at about 10° intervals in longitude as decade-markers and as hour-markers and to the Babylonian use of twelve constellations centred on the Ecliptic to mark the Sun's annual progress. The details of the three schemes are, of course, quite different.

Just as the Babylonians *circa* 400 BC substituted schematic 30° segments of the Ecliptic for the original twelve zodiacal constellations somewhat variant in longitudinal extent, so the Hindus perhaps early in the first millennium AD substituted, while preserving the names, 27 segments each 13° 20′ in extent, thus constituting schematic *nakshatras*. Each of these was divided into four *pada* of 3° 20′. It may be noticed that two schematic *nakshatras* plus one *pada*, that is 13° 20′ + 13° 20′ + 3° 20′, equals one Babylonian Sign of 30° in extent. When the Indians ultimately borrowed the Babylonian Signs (the Sanskrit word for Sign is *Rasi*), the Sign named *Mesha* (Sanskrit for ram) was equated to the *nakshatra* segments *Asvini* and *Bharani* plus the first *pada* of *Krittika* and the Sign named *Vrishabha* (Sanskrit for bull) was equated to the three remaining *pada* of *Krittika*, the whole of *Rohini* and the first two *pada* of *Mrigasiras*, and so on.

The Babylonian convention of the twelve Signs apparently reached India through a Greek intermediary for, as we have seen, in addition to Sanskrit translations there were also in use corruptions of the Greek names. I have already reported another Indian importation from Babylonia with a modification, namely the use of the sexagesimal fractions for the subdivision of the day into sixty *ghati* periods, of the *ghati* into sixty *pala* periods and so on, and another from a Hellenistic Greek source, namely the 7-day week with planetary day names.

Though the use of twenty-seven or twenty-eight *nakshatras* shows a concern with the sidereal month of about 27.32 days, there is early evidence of a concern with the synodic month of about 29.53 days. Possibly a rounding up of some early estimate of this value led to the Vedic schematic months of 30 days, which of course would have soon got out of step with the phases of the Moon. After 12 schematic months of 30 days, the first day of the schematic month would occur about 6 days after the beginning of the synodic month, and after 32 schematic months about 15 days after it. Later, the Hindus established more accurate lunar months (each called *chandra masa*) of 29 or 30 days in rough alternation and tied to the phases of the Moon. They were measured in some regions from new Moon to new Moon (conjunction) and in others from full Moon to full Moon. Even today the former practice prevails generally in Southern India and the latter in the North. Such lunar months were divided into two periods called *paksha* (wing), the *sukla* (white or bright) *paksha* of the waxing Moon and *krishna* (black or dark) *paksha* of the waning Moon. These lunar months derived their names from the *nakshatra* segment in which their full Moon usually occurred. Thus, the lunar month (*chandra masa*) name *Karttika* comes from *Krittika*, *Margrasirsha* from *Mrigasiras*, *Pausha* from *Pushya* and so on, the former of each pair being an adjectival form of the latter noun form.

Each *paksha* of these lunar months was divided into fifteen periods, each a *tithi* which may be thought of as a 'lunar day'. Each *tithi* was the period required for the angular separation in longitude of the Sun and the Moon to change by 12°. The first *tithi* of *sukla paksha* began when the two bodies were in conjunction (new Moon), the second when the Moon had moved 12° ahead of the Sun, the third when the separation was 24° and so on. Because of variations in the apparent velocities of the Sun and, especially, of the Moon, the *tithi* periods are of variable duration. Sometimes, when the Sun is running fastest and the Moon slowest, they are longer than a day (24 hours) but on average they are less, namely 23 hours 37 minutes and 28.09 seconds. Each *tithi* has its own name, essentially an ordinal number—*pratipad*, *divitiya*, *tritiya*, *chaturthi* and so on. The fifteenth *tithi* in the *sukla paksha* is called *purnima* (full Moon) and in the *krishna paksha*, *amavasya* (new Moon). Each *tithi* is divided into two periods, each called a *karana*. The Babylonians used for certain purposes lunar 'days' which were thirtieths of the lunar month (see Neugebauer, 1969) and the Indians may have derived the *tithi* periods from them.

At some time in the first half of the first millennium AD, the Babylonian Signs of the Zodiac having been adopted in India and the tropical year having been recognized as being about 365.25 days in duration, a system of 'solar months' was instituted. Each of these, called a *saura* (solar) *masa*, was marked by the entry (*sankranti*) of the Sun into a Sign. For example, *Meshasankranti* was the entry of the Sun into *Aries* and *Vrishabhasankranti* was its entry into *Taurus*. As a result of the varying apparent velocity of the Sun, these solar months were rounded 29 days (2 or 3 of them), 30 days (5 or 4 of them), 31 days (4 of them) and 32 days (1 of them) in duration. They totalled 365 days and 366 days in the ratio of about 3:1. Special emphasis was placed on *Meshasankranti*, *Karkasankranti*, *Tulasankranti* and *Makarasankranti*, the four equinoctial and solstitial points. Perhaps at the time when this system began the true equinoctial and solstitial points were used (or close approximations to them), but subsequently for calendrical purposes the precession of the equinoxes was ignored, the values being frozen for about the fourth or fifth century AD. Sewell and Dikshit (1896, p. 9) claim about AD 450, whereas *The Indian Ephemeris and Nautical Almanac for the Year* 1967 (p. 389) claims about AD 285; the difference in dating amounting to about 2° in longitude. For some astronomical purposes the shift of the equinoxes (*sa-ayana*, with movement) was taken into account, but for the calendrical purposes just discussed the assumption was 'without movement' (*nirayana*) of the First Point of Aries.

When the solar months were first adopted they tended to take the name of the Sign, entry into which by the Sun governed their beginnings. Later, however, it became customary to call them by the same name as that of the lunar months with which they were roughly coincident, thus *saura Chaitra* was roughly coincident with *chandra Chaitra*, *saura Vaisakha* with *chandra Vaisakha* and so on. The solar months having thus annexed the lunar months' names, they came to govern the application of the lunar month names. Thus, in one system *chandra Chaitra* is not so-called because its full Moon occurs in the schematic *nakshatra Chaitra* but because the *saura Chaitra* (beginning with the *Meshasankranti*) includes its beginning. This practice led either to the repetition occasionally of a *chandra masa* name with the qualifying *adhika* (added) or *divitiya* (second) or to its omission. Briefly, if a solar month had a lunar month beginning very early in it and another late in it, the second was called the *adhika* (or *divitiya*) lunar month of the same name as the first. On rarer occasions when no lunar month began in the solar month, the name of the solar month concerned was skipped in the succession of lunar months. The shortest solar month is 29 days, so it is possible for one of the longer 30-day lunar months wholly to include it.

Though a conjunction or opposition of the Sun and the Moon or an entry into a Sign by the Sun occurs at a particular time within a day and though the Indians were quite skilful in calculating these events by the second half of the first millennium AD (see Sewell, 1924), it is more convenient for calendar-makers using these events for their purposes to select a rounded or whole day. In most cases the Hindus used the day, deemed to begin at sunrise, on which the event occurred as the first day of the *chandra masa* or *saura masa*, though there were some regional variations; further if the event were late in the day beginning at sunrise they often placed the beginning of the month on the next day.

Possibly towards the end of the first millennium AD, a civil calendar using schematic solar months was introduced. The first civil month *Chaitra* begins usually on the day after that on which the Spring Equinox or *Meshasankranti* (allowing for precession) occurs. It has 30 days in ordinary years and 31 in leap-years occurring every fourth year. The following 5 civil months—*Vaisakha*, *Jyaistha*, *Ashadha*, *Sravana* and *Bhadrapada*—each have 31 days, and the remaining 6—*Asvina*, *Karttika*, *Margasirsha*, *Pausha*, *Magha* and *Phalguna*—each have 30 days. There are some similarities here to the later Iranian National Calendar.

From this time forward a complex calendar with lunar months, solar months and schematic solar months running in some sort of parallel, but with regional differences in the detailed practices including that of naming the months, was maintained. There was no great problem in keeping in parallel the *saura masa* reckoned from the day of the Sun's entry into the frozen Signs (that is those calculated without allowance for precession) and the civil months of predetermined durations governed roughly by the Sun's entries into the 'true' Signs, as the latter lags only a little behind the former (7 or 8 days at the present time). The lunar months provide a greater difficulty. Twelve of them total only 354 or 355 days, so every now and then a *chandra masa* name has to be repeated or to be suppressed in the manner indicated above.

In order to illustrate in a more concrete way some of the points I have been making let me cite some data extracted from *The Indian Ephemeris and Nautical Almanac for the Year* 1967. On 14 March (Gregorian) 1967, the Sun entered the old *Mesha* (that is the Sign *Aries* calculated without allowance for the precession of the equinoxes) and the *saura Chaitra* began on that day. On 21 March the Sun entered the true *Mesha*, (that is, *Aries* calculated with allowance for the precession) and on the following day the civil *Chaitra* began. On 9 April, the Sun and the Moon were in conjunction and *chandra Chaitra* began. Some 11 months later (in 1968), on 12 February, the Sun entered the old *Mina* and the *saura Phalguna* began. On 19 February, the Sun entered the true *Mina* and on the following day civil *Phalguna* began. On 28 February a new Moon occurred and *chandra Phalguna* began. The interval between solar and civil month beginnings was in both cases 7 days (in about half the months it is 8) whereas in the 11 months the interval between the *saura* and the *chandra* month beginnings

103

decreased from 26 to 16 days. It is obvious that if the *chandra* month beginning is to be prevented from getting ahead of the beginning of the like-named *saura* month, a *chandra* month name would have to be repeated in about 18 months from the *Phalguna* set of months just examined, perhaps an *adhika Ashadha* or an *adhika Sravanna* (in 1969). Further when a 30-day *chandra masa* happens to straddle the 29-day *saura masa Phalguna*, presumably a rare event, a *chandra masa* name will have to be suppressed.

I have already referred to the 5-year *yuga* cycle which was used in at least late Vedic times as a basis for the intercalation of an extra month. Sometime in the mid-first millennium AD, when so many Babylonian-Hellenistic conventions were being adopted, the Metonic cycle was for a time used for the intercalation of needed additional lunar months. After the introduction of the solar months the Metonic cycle was replaced by the system which I have described above of adding or suppressing a lunar month. This seems to have been an Indian invention.

I shall mention as a curiosity, but not examine, a very long cycle, the *Kaliyuga*, used in a mid-first millennium AD work the *Suryasiddhanta*, one of a series of five classical *siddhantas*, or works on astronomically determined periods (see Sewell, 1924). The period was 432000 years and was based on a calculation back to a time when the Sun, the Moon and the five other naked eye planets were allegedly all in conjunction in 3102 BC.

I should like to report in some detail another Indian period longer than a year and with a sounder empirical basis than either the Vedic *yuga* or the later *Kaliyuga*. The sidereal period of Jupiter is 4332.6 days or about 11.86 years. Consequently about each year Jupiter moves into a new Sign of the Zodiac, completing the Circle of the Beasts in about 12 years. Hence, for a time the Hindus named the year in which Jupiter was in a given Sign with a modification of the *nakshatra* name which the solar month had when the Sun was in that Sign, thus *Mahachaitra*, *Mahavaisakha*, *Mahajyaistha* and so on, the prefix *maha* meaning great, as in *Maharajah*. We shall later find a similar duodenary Jupiter cycle in a context of sexagenary cycles in Chinese calendrical practices. I have no clue to the historical relations between the two practices; they may be coincidences, one may have been the source of the other, or they may have had a common outside source. Where similar calendrical practices in different and remote communities are based on some establishable astronomical periods one should not too readily reject the possibility of independent discovery; where the practices are more conventional or arbitrary, for example, the 7-day week, one should be more eager to look for borrowings by one community from another. The Indians were considerable borrowers, but they were also creative even in respect of their borrowings.

A more generally used Indian Jupiter cycle consisted of five of the duodenary cycles just described, generating a sexagenary cycle. In this 60-year cycle, each year had a special name, for example *prabhava*, *vibhava*, *sukla*, *pramoda* and so on (see Renou and Filliozat). As the entry of Jupiter into successive Signs is about 4.19 days less than the tropical year, after about 88 Jupiter Sign-entries or about 87 tropical years, Jupiter enters a Sign early in a tropical year and enters the next Sign before that year ends. On these occasions Jupiter is said to jump a Sign and the special name in the sexagenary set is suppressed.

In addition to the variations in the basic Hindu calendar which I have been describing, there were at least until recently many eras in use. Earlier the Vikrama Era beginning from 57 BC seems to have been the one most favoured; later the Saka Era, beginning from AD 78 seems to have replaced it in favour. But there have been and are many others, most confined mainly to a particular geographical region. In indicating the place of a year in an era there has been a marked but not universal tendency to give the number of the expired, that is preceding, year and not that of the current year. We indicate the day, the month and the year we are in but we refer to the elapsed hour within the half day. Thus we write 10.15 a.m., 15 January AD 1973, meaning that we are a quarter way through the eleventh hour after midnight within the fifteenth day of January within the year 1973 of the Christian Era. Indian practice usually referred to the completed or elapsed year in the Era being used. We shall find the same principle in use among the Meso-Americans even in respect of the day of their 20-day *uinal*.

It would not be proper to omit mention of the Indian almanac called the *panchanga* (the five limbs) which is important for astrological purposes. It gives the time and date of the beginning (or the end) of: (i) each day in the 7-day week borrowed from Hellenistic sources; (ii) each *tithi*, the thirtieth fraction of the Moon's advance from the Sun, probably borrowed or adapted from Babylonia; (iii) the Moon's entry into each schematic *nakshatra*, perhaps an indigenous convention but possibly borrowed from China or from Babylonia; (iv) each *yoga* derived from the sum of the Sun's and the Moon's longitude from the First Point in Aries, the sum being divided into 27 equal parts, each with its own name (this may well have been an indigenous convention); and (v) each *karana* or half *tithi*.

I have tried to avoid going into astrological thought except where it has been apparently influential on calendrical practice. The belief that the stars, especially the wanderers, had an influence on human destiny (as distinct from marking out the seasons and other important intervals of time) may well have had its origin in Babylonia. But as I have said the predominant Babylonian conception of this celestial influence was on the community as a whole and on the King (see nevertheless Sachs, 1952a, indicating a development of the notion of influence on ordinary persons). In the decline of Egypt in the late first millennium BC these notions of stellar influences on individual human destiny seem to have become popular but it was among the Hellenistic Greeks and the Romans, perhaps among the lower classes in the central Empire and among the conquered peoples in the outlying provinces where it flourished and was elaborated (see Cumont, 1912). Astrology enjoyed great attention in Europe during the Middle Ages, despite its basic incongruity with Christian beliefs. One may cite Chaucer's concern with it in his later writings. Sweeping through Hellenistic Greece and the near Middle East, it found a nutritious environment alongside Babylonian astronomical conventions in India. Though it has had a resurgence in the West, partly in crude evening newspaper columns in the mid-twentieth century, it has persisted in the Indian sub-continent with careful calculations of an astronomical sort which would be quite beyond the ken of the Western newspaper writer of the good and bad news for a Gemini or a Capricorn.

I have explored only a limited number of the complexities and regional variations of Indian calendrical practices. I have tried to keep my account to a thumb-nail sketch depicting the main features and hinting at the variations. For those who wish to explore the complexities and the variations I recommend Sewell and Dikshit (1896), Sewell (1912), Sewell (1924), de Saussure (1919 and 1920) and Renou and Filliozat (1953). Indeed, a lot can be learned from a modern *Indian Ephemeris and Nautical Almanac*.

10/THE CHINESE CALENDAR

The Chinese probably began some millennia BC to reckon the passage of time by days and by approximate lunar synodic months. After a time, as 12 such months got out of step with the seasons, they seem, like the inhabitants of early Mesopotamia, to have let in every now and then an embolistic year with a thirteenth or intercalary month. By the thirteenth century BC they appear to have worked out that the year was about 365.25 days and the synodic month about 29.53 days, better values perhaps than those arrived at by any contemporaries in other places. By the early part of the first millennium AD they had 365.242815 days for the tropical year, 365.255989 days for the sidereal year and 29.530585 days for the synodic month (see Needham, 1959), again values nearer the mark than those used elsewhere at that time.

From at least 104 BC, when the Emporer Wei-ti instituted a revised calendar, and possibly for a few centuries before, the Chinese had a luni-solar calendar basically like the Babylonian standardized calendar which was adopted in the early fourth century BC. There were many official variations in the calendar from 104 BC until AD 1912 when the Gregorian calendar was adopted by the new Republic, but the changes were relatively minor. This calendar had months (*yüeh*) of 29 or 30 days in rough alternation (a system going back no doubt to the second millennium BC); it had ordinary years of 12 months and so of 354 or less commonly 355 days and embolistic years with an intercalary month (*jun yüeh*) and so of 383, 384 or 385 days. The Chinese embolistic year, as in the Babylonian standardized calendar, occurred seven times in a cycle of 19 years and in about the same positions within the cycle as in Babylonia, namely the third, the fifth or the sixth, the eighth, the eleventh, the thirteenth or fourteenth, the sixteenth or the seventeenth and the nineteenth years. The cycle of 19 years and 235 lunar months was called *chang* (the Metonic cycle of the West). In rounded days it totalled 6940 days which was about two-fifths of a day longer than 19 tropical years at that time and 235 lunations which of course did not quite match. Later, perhaps early in the first millennium AD, a longer cycle *pu* (four *chang* cycles with 1 day left out of one of them) was introduced. Such a *pu* cycle was only 0.6 day longer than 76 tropical years. It was the same as the cycle proposed by Kallippos *circa* 334 BC. These similarities suggest a borrowing by one set of calendar-makers from the other, in which case history suggests that the Babylonians and perhaps the Greeks had temporal priority. Careful observers, recorders and analysts could, of course, arrive at all these matters independently and the Chinese may well have done so.

There are some differences between Babylonian and Chinese calendrical systems which should be noted. First, whereas the Babylonians began the year with the new Moon (strictly, in their case, the first visible crescent after sunset) about the time of the Spring Equinox, the Chinese began it with the new Moon mid-way between the Winter Solstice and the Spring Equinox. Second, whereas the Babylonian calendar let in the intercalary month usually after the twelfth month (though occasionally after the sixth), the Chinese let it in after various non-Winter months in accordance with a rule which will be explained later.

There are similarities and differences in the arbitrary divisions of the day by the Babylonians and the Chinese. At one time, as we have seen, the Babylonians divided the day (reckoned from sunset) into twelve equal divisions, each a *beru* (they later substituted the Egyptian 24 'temporal hours'), and the Chinese from the fourth century BC divided the day (ordinarily reckoned from midnight but for this operation from 11 p.m.) into twelve equal *shih* periods. However, whereas the Babylonians divided the *beru* into sixtieths and that fraction into further sixtieths, the Chinese divided the *shih* into eighths called *kho*, equal to 15 minutes of our time. The Chinese also divided the day into hundredths, each also called a *kho*, but which were 14 minutes 24 seconds of our time.

At a very early date, at least early in the first millennium BC, the Chinese divided the Equator into twenty-four segments, each 15° of longitude in extent. The period taken by the Sun to traverse such a segment is called a *chhi*. It averages 15.23 days but because of the variable apparent velocity of the Sun (least in the northern Summer and greatest in the northern Winter) the period may be as long as about 15.74 days or as short as about 14.72 days. The Chinese rounded the periods to whole days to produce five or six *chhi* of 16 days and nineteen or eighteen of 15 days. Those *chhi* usually spanning the middle of a lunar month were called *chung-chhi* (*chung* is 'middle') and those usually spanning the ends of neighbouring months were *chieh-chhi* (*chieh* is 'nodal' or 'at a junction'). Each *chhi* had its own name, thus *Li-chhun* (the beginning of Spring) was the period during which the Sun was between 315° and 330° of Equatorial longitude, that is, at least approximately, in the second half of the Western sign *Aquarius*; *Yu-shui* (the rains) when the Sun was between 330° and 345°, that is, in the first half of *Pisces*; *Ching-chih* (awakening of insects) when the Sun was between 345° and 360°, that is, the second half of *Pisces*; *Chung-fen* (Spring Equinox) when the Sun was between 360°(0°) and 15°, that is, the first half of *Aries*; and so on. The *chhi* system was very early in origin, say second millennium BC (see Needham, 1959) and so predated the Near Eastern Zodiacal signs of 30° extent. Much later, about AD 600, pairs of 15° segments were combined to form signs of the Zodiac which had by then been borrowed from Babylonia through India but given distinctive Chinese animal names which had been used for other duodenary cycles.

The new year began with the new Moon nearest to the beginning of *Li-chhun* which occurred on or about 5 February (Gregorian). As a month is 29 or 30 days, New Year's Day occurred between about 20 January and 19 February. After an ordinary year of 354 or 355 days, New Year's Day moved forward about 11 days in terms of Gregorian dates. When it moved forward to a date between 20 January and 30 January, the year so beginning had to be embolistic (otherwise the following year would begin with the new Moon next but one nearest the beginning of *Li-chhun*). It is this rule which determines which years in the 19-year cycle are embolistic. Further the intercalary month in the embolistic year is that one which ended before the beginning of a *chieh-chhi* (information from Professor Ho Peng-yoke). This could be any of the non-winter months as the *chhi* tend to be shortest in winter but it would most likely be a summer month when the *chhi* tend to be longest. This rule for selecting the intercalary month is similar in principle to that used by the Hindus in selecting their intercalary *chandra masa*; it is likely, however, to have yielded a slightly different result as the Hindus were using Signs 30° in extent and were anchoring them to a fixed and not a precessing First Point of Aries; the Chinese located the beginning of *Chung-fen* at the precessing First Point of Aries.

I have stated above, following my various authorities but particularly Needham (1959) and de Saussure (1920) on this occasion, that the Chinese lunar month began with the new Moon. In modern astronomical usage 'new Moon' refers to the conjunction, yet one may reasonably imagine watchers for the first visible crescent, such as the Babylonians, the Greeks, the early Romans and the Jews, not to mention some other Semitic peoples, referring to that apparition as the new Moon, as we tend to do. The early Egyptians by contrast used the day (ending at dawn) of the last visible crescent before sunrise as the last day of the lunar calendar month and began the new month on the next day. The term 'new Moon' can thus have several meanings: the first visible crescent, the conjunction or even the disappearance of the 'old Moon'. I have sought to establish, with no great success, what criterion the Chinese used for the beginning of the lunar calendar months. I suspect that there were changes with the passage of time.

The Chinese engaged in a great deal of minor tinkering with their calendar over the two millennia for which we have records. Professor Ho Peng-Yoke kindly extracted for me some relevant information given in *Li-fa t'ung-chih* written by Chu Wen-hsin and not yet translated into English. From 104 BC when the Emperor Wei-ti reformed the existing lunar or perhaps luni-solar calendar there were until its official replacement in AD 1912 by the Gregorian calendar forty-two further reforms, not to mention many regional variants. Professor Ho Peng-Yoke says that in the Chinese mind to promulgate a calendar is exercise the right of a ruler. Chu Wen-hsin in addition to giving the dates of introduction of the forty-two variants of the *T'ai-ch'u* calendar produced by or for Wei-ti in 104 BC (some lasted only a couple of decades and others a couple of centuries) also states the average duration of the years in each. Quite early the years approximated on average 365.25 days but the average shrank, in zig-zag fashion, to about 365.2423 days in the mid-seventeenth century. I suspect that the criterion for the first day of the month may also have changed from time to time.

Sivin (1969) cites two early first millennium AD treatises which dealt with the beginning of the month. The first discussing the calendar prior to 104 BC says that 'the new moon visible on the last day of the calendar month and the old moon visible on the first day are omens of the ruler's laxity or overstrictness'. I am inclined to interpret this as meaning that the first day of the calendar month should have occurred on a day between those on which the old moon was visible (before sunrise) and the new moon was visible (after sunset), but it may have some other implication. The second treatise quoted by Sivin speaking of the *T' ai-ch'u* calendar of Wei-ti says

The calendar ran slightly behind the phenomena so that the new moon occurred earlier than the calendar predicted. The conjunction would take place on the last day of the month in some cases and the moon would appear on the first day in other cases.

To check what might be happening in the *Kuei-mao* calendar (AD 1742 to 1911), I took more or less at random a run of 26 months from 2 December 1880 as set out in *A Sino-Western Calendar for Two Thousand Years: 1–2000 AD* by Hsueh Chung-san and Ou-yang I (1955). I compared the dates of the first days of these 26 months as given in that work with the times and dates of conjunction (converted to 'Peking Mean Time') as set out in *The Nautical Almanac* for the years 1880, 1881 and 1882. Eleven of these Chinese months began on the day of conjunction, 15 on the day after but none of the day before (the day being reckoned from midnight). On eight of the eleven occasions when the first calendar month day coincided with the day of conjunction, conjunction occurred before midday in 'Peking Mean Time'; on twelve of the fifteen occasions when the first day of the month occurred on the day after conjunction, conjunction occurred after midday. There is an obvious tendency here, akin to one to be found in Indian calendrical practice. There are, however, some fairly marked departures from the tendency, for example 27 May 1881 was the first day of a calendar month although the conjunction occurred at about 3.50 p.m. on that day and 20 June 1882 was the first day of a calendar month although the conjunction occurred at about 8.05 a.m. on the day before. Further using data from *The Nautical Almanac* for the relevant year I had no difficulty in generating months of roughly alternating 29 and 30 days with their first days on the day of conjunction. At this time the Chinese would have had data almost as precise as those in *The Nautical Almanac*, certainly good enough for this purpose It is almost as though the Chinese at this time in trying to avoid under-shooting the day of conjunction quite often over-shot it. There is, however, another possibility. They may have been aiming at the first visible crescent. To check this possibility I worked out from a table in *Norton's Star Atlas and Reference Book* times of sunset in Peking on the first days of the 26 calendar months, and in a qualitative way tried to estimate the probability of a visible crescent after sunset on the first day of these calendar months. I took into account the obliquity of the Ecliptic to the horizon, the latitude of the Moon and the rapidity with which the Moon was separating from the Sun. I concluded that on one occasion there was very probably, perhaps certainly, a first visible crescent after sunset on the first day of the calendar month, that on 2 or 3 other first days a first visible crescent was possible but that on the remaining 22 or 23 first days of the month a first visible crescent was impossible or highly improbable. On no first day could there have been a last visible crescent before sunrise on the first day of the calendar month.

All the foregoing is better evidence for the day of conjunction, if the conjunction is early in the day, or the day after, if the conjunction is late in its day, than it is for the first visible crescent. It is all fairly clear evidence against the day after the last visible crescent as the first day of the calendar month.

Emboldened by the exercise just described, I dipped back much earlier into the data in *A Sino-European Calendar for Two Thousand Years*. The data for the first century AD have many gaps and hence seemed suspect as well as not readily usable. The data for the late second century seemed more confidently stated (though, of course, this does not mean that they were more accurate). No issues of *The Nautical Almanac* were available for the epoch but Bickerman provides appropriate dates and times of conjunction. Bickerman's data have been obtained by projection back from modern data on rules which have been improved since they were used to generate his data; this may well be a weakness in my next exercise. My comparisons were necessarily much rougher than for the period 1880–2. I had no data on the Moon's position north or south of the Ecliptic nor on the rate at which the Moon was separating from the Sun. Hence I constructed a nomograph, see Fig. 10.1, based on Schoch's values for Babylon but adapted for the latitude of Peking and incorporating in a somewhat qualitative way variations arising from other relevant considerations. It would require a page or two to set out fully the considerations which entered into the making of this nomograph. It was so rough that I do not believe that the use of space would be justified. More important to mention is the result of its application to the 1880–2 data already investigated. The nomograph gave essentially the same results as my earlier more careful investigation, though slightly more generous in respect of probable and possible first crescents on the first day of the month.

I took for investigation two runs of 25 months beginning on 16 January AD 150 and on 21 January AD 155. I concluded that there were perhaps fourteen occasions when there was probably a first visible crescent on the first day of the month, sixteen occasions when there

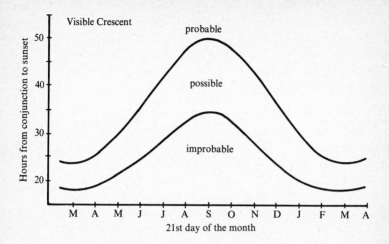

Fig 10.1   Nomograph constructed for estimating the likelihood of a
first visible crescent at certain intervals between conjunction and
sunset and for various times within the year, at the latitude of Peking.
The band of 'possible' first visible crescents allow for the occurrence of
some unfavourable conditions, for example, the Moon being south of
the Ecliptic, whereas the band of 'probables' assumes all conditions are
favourable.

was a possible first visible crescent, twenty occasions when a first
visible crescent was highly improbable or impossible and no occasion
on which there could have been a last visible crescent before sunrise on
that day. If these inferences are correct it would seem that the Chinese
in the second century AD were using either the day of the predicted
but not observed first visible crescent and often undershooting it or
the day of conjunction and often overshooting it.

Sivin's reports and my two dubious studies suggest to me, and I
should not wish to use a stronger word, (i) that the Chinese for at least
some two millennia or more were aiming at the day of conjunction,
(ii) that at first they tolerated but with some dismay both last visible
and first visible crescents on the first day of the calendar month,
(iii) later they became intolerant of last visible crescents on that day
and (iv) still later they tried to minimize first visible crescents but suffer-
ed a few of them in preference to undershooting the day of conjunction.
Perhaps in this last suggested phase they used the rule 'First day of the

calendar month if the conjunction is before midday and next day if it is after midday' but through inadequacies of data or obsessions about alternating months of 29 or 30 days (which I doubt) or on some other considerations (which I have not been able to locate) sometimes broke the rule.

I should now like to turn to some cycles of years other than the *chang* cycle of 19 years (like the Metonic cycle) and the *pu* cycle of 76 years (like the cycle proposed by Kallipos). These were based on considerations other than those of adjusting a lunar year to the tropical year by periodic intercalary months.

First, the Chinese had a duodenary cycle of years based, like that in India, on Jupiter's progress among the fixed stars. As Jupiter's sidereal period is 11.86 years, the planet moves eastward each tropical year about 30.354°. This is slightly greater than a Babylonian Sign of the Zodiac. Each of the 12 Jupiter years was given one of the names of the twelve 'terrestrial branches' which I shall discuss below and which were also bestowed on the Signs of the Zodiac when they were adopted very much later.

Second, they had a sexagenary cycle not based on five Jupiter cycles as in India and not confined to the years. Indeed it seems to have been employed first, in perhaps the late second millennium BC, for a cycle of days and was not applied to the years until near the end of the first millennium BC. The manner of its generation is peculiar (though the same principle of generating a cycle is to be found in the Meso-American calendars). Successive items in two lists, the ten 'celestial stems' (*chih*) and the twelve 'terrestrial branches' (*kan*), are paired. Let capital letters stand for the members of the *chih* list, thus A, B, C, D, ..., J, and minuscules for the members of the *kan* list, thus a, b, c, d, ..., l. Then a sixty-item set of pairs may be generated to produce

Aa, Bb, Cc, Dd, Ee, Ff, Gg, Hh, Ii, Jj
Ak, Bl, Ca, Db, Ec, Fd, Ge, Hf, Ig, Jh
Ai, Bj, Ck, Dl, Ea, Fb, Gc, Hd, Ie, Jf
and so on.

The sixtieth pair is *Jl* and the sixty-first *Aa* thus beginning a new cycle.

According to Needham (1959) the origins of the *chih* and the *kan* lists are obscure. He suggests that the former may have begun as the names of the 10-day period (obtained by dividing the 'full' lunar month into thirds). The latter seem to have been associated with the 12 lunar months which almost make up a year, with the twelve *shih* into which the day is divided and later with the 12 years in the Jupiter cycle. I shall list the twelve *kan* with the animal names in Chinese and English long associated with them.

Tzu (rat), *chhou* (ox), *yin* (tiger), *mao* (hare), *chhen* (dragon), *ssu* (snake), *wu* (horse), *wei* (sheep), *shen* (monkey), *yu* (cock), *hsii* (dog) and *hai* (pig).

In accordance with this list the Chinese have: (i) the 'hour' (strictly double hour or *shih*) of the rat, of the ox, of the tiger and so on; (ii) the day of the rat, of the ox, of the tiger and so on, qualified by the appropriate *chih* term in the sexagenary cycle, thus *chia-tzu* or *i-tzu* or *ping-tzu*, for days which are 12 apart; (iii) the month of the rat, of the ox, and so on, although they are more usually known as the first, the second, the third and so on month of the year; and (iv) the year of the rat, of the ox and so on, though they were also known as the first, the second, the third and so on year of some named Emperor's reign.

Twelve double hours (*shih*) make a day. A sexagenary cycle of days comes close to 2 lunar synodic months rounded to 29 or 30 days (say 59 days for the pair). A sexagenary cycle of months comes out to rather less than 5 years, assuming that intercalation is being employed. A sexagenary cycle of years (averaging about 365.25 days) comes out a little longer (21914.5 days) than five Jupiter cycles (21662.95 days). Perhaps these near coincidences (the deviations of which would not be so evident at first) were enough to convince the early Chinese calendar-makers that the sexagenary cycles could be applied to the days, the months and the years. Whatever be the case they applied them. It would be roughly analogous were we to say the Sun hour of the Moon day of the Twia-month of the Woden year or the *Januarius* hour of the *Februarius* day of the *Martius* month of the *Aprilis* year or better still the *Aries* hour of the *Taurus* day of the *Gemini* month of the *Cancer* year.

Though this very ancient calendar was officially abolished on the establishment of the Republic of China in AD 1912, it lingered on in China and in Chinese communities abroad.

The Chinese calendar in its basic form has had a slightly longer run than the essentially Roman calendar which we use, though both have had a shorter run than the Egyptian civil calendar especially if we count its continued modified forms among the Copts and Ethiopians, among the Persians and among the Parsees in India. Calendars are hard both to make and to unmake, partly because conventions and traditions are so important in them whatever hard core of adjusted astronomical fact they have in them.

It is difficult to distinguish independent creations and borrowings when comparing practices in the Far East and the Near East. There are clear instances of borrowings, sometimes through India but sometimes along the trade-route north of India. The concept of the Zodiac almost certainly moved from the Near East to the Far East through India. Gunpowder and silk came from China to the West through the Near East perhaps on the northern route. The seven-day planetary week came temporarily into China from Hellenistic sources possibly through India but perhaps through the northern route from northern Persian regions. Sunday in the short-lived Chinese week was *Mit*, possibly from Mithra, the Sun god. The 360° division of the circle also seems to have drifted from Mesopotamia, though in China it was corrected for a time to 365.25°, on the assumption that it was based on average daily rate of the Sun's progress amongst the fixed stars. There is clear evidence of Chinese innovation. As I have claimed the Chinese could easily have discovered the Metonic Cycle without influence from the Near East. It is also important to recognize that while astronomers in the Near East, including the Greeks, and in India adopted an orientation for celestial location based on the Ecliptic, the Chinese from the outset adopted an orientation based on the Celestial Equator and Poles, the reference frame now adopted internationally by astronomers.

11/MESO-AMERICAN CALENDARS

I shall conclude my account of specific historical calendar systems with a brief examination of a set of Meso-American calendars, originating it would seem with the Maya perhaps late in the first millennium BC, developed by them to a peak of elaboration in the first millennium AD and then spreading north into Mexico where the Spaniards first found it in use among the Aztecs. I include it for several reasons. First, it was perhaps the most sophisticated and elaborate calendar outside the Mediterranean-Asian area to which I have already devoted my attention. Indeed, in some ways the Meso-American set constitutes a *tour-de-force* in calendar-making. Second, it reveals a people even more in the grip of a number system than any I have so far described. Third, in some respects it resembles Egyptian and in some other respects Chinese calendrical practices. This has led some scholars to suggest that the Maya were Egyptian or Chinese migrants or at any rate that they had been influenced by such migrants. I seriously doubt these suggestions but I leave it to my readers to make their own inquiries and to draw their own conclusions.

I shall begin with a brief account of the Meso-American number system. As we have seen the Egyptian, the Indian and the Chinese number systems were decimal and the Mesopotarian was sexagesimal; the Roman number was basically decimal though it recognized special intermediate marker points at 5, 50 and 500. The Meso-American number system was vigesimal, counting to the first 20, then to 20×20 (400), then to $20 \times 20 \times 20$ (8000) and so on. Though there were hints of a positional placement of the numerals in the Roman notation (large values ahead of smaller values except in cases such as IX) the Mesopotamian and Hindu notations were the most clearly positional among those already cited. The Meso-American system was equally positional. Dots were used for one to four, a stroke for five, a stroke and a dot for six, two strokes for ten, three strokes and four dots for nineteen. For twenty a shell or some other symbol of emptiness was written in the first place and a dot in the second (or twenties) place, see Fig. 11.1.

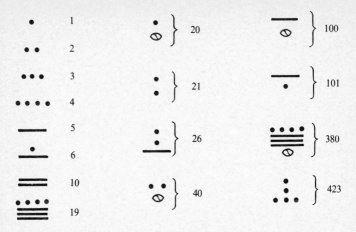

Fig 11.1   The Meso-American numerals set out in vertical places in
the second and third columns. The first entry in the second column is
to be read 'one 20 and no units', the second 'one 20 and one unit', and
the third 'one 20 and six units'. The last entry in the third column is
'one (20 x 20), one 20 and three units'.

Using this system the Meso-Americans could go up from units almost
ad infinitum. At any rate they went up to hundreds of millions.

The Mesopotamians could as we have seen move down in their
sexagesimal fractions also almost *ad infinitum*. The Hindus using
Mesopotamian sexagesimal fractions added to their decimal system
for quantities of unit value and above could do likewise but with a
change of base. The Egyptians with their added unit fractions, e.g.,
(one-half + one-quarter, for three-quarters) were more handicapped
and the Romans with their tenths and later twelfths were still more
handicapped. Though the Meso-Americans were so clever with
multiples, they never seem to have got more than the faintest notion of
fractions. 'Incomplete' or 'about half complete' were about as far as
they got, although some of their calculations expressed as multiples
imply fractions which they seem to have been unable to express; I
shall report some cases later.

The Hindus, as we have learned, had a tendency to report elapsed or
completed years just as we report elapsed hours and minutes. We
report the day, the month and the year in which we are. The Meso-
Americans had a tendency to report the elapsed day and the elapsed

Ik	*Manik*	*Eb*	*Caban*
Akbal	*Lamat*	*Ben*	*Eznab*
Kan	*Muluc*	*Ix*	*Cauac*
Chicchan	*Oc*	*Men*	*Ahau*
Cimi	*Chuen*	*Cib*	*Imix*

Table 11.1   The Yucatec names of the 20 Maya days. To be read in order down the columns from left to right.

year. They had 20-day periods (each a *uinal*) sometimes referred to as 'months'. The first day of this period was its enthronement or seating and the second day in our conception its first day in theirs (that is the day after the first completed day). Were we to write 2 February 1973 in their convention we would write 1 (completed) February (uncompleted) 1972 (completed).

We shall find in the many periods used in the Meso-American calendrical schemes something approaching an obsession with the number 20 (see Thompson, 1950, or for a brief account Morley and Brainerd, 1963). Perhaps it will be best to report first a cycle of 260 days, called by the Maya in the Yucatec language the *tzolkin,* the count of the days (*kin* being a day). It was generated on a principle similar to that by which the Chinese sexagenary cycle was generated. In the Mayan case the numbers 1 to 13 were used to represent the thirteen gods of the upper world (there were also nine gods of the lower world). Each day in a cycle of twenty had its own name, *Ik, Akbal, Kan, ...,* *Ahau* and *Imix* (see Table 11.1) the numbers and names were successively paired thus 1 *Ik*, 2 *Akbal*, 3 *Kan*, ..., 13 *Ix*, 1 *Men*, ..., 6 *Ahau*, 7 *Imix*, 8 *Ik*, 9 *Akbal* and so on until the 260th pair 13 *Imix* had been reached and the *tzolkin* completed. The next pair 1 *Ik* began the next 260-day count. This cycle was used primarily for religious ceremonial purposes.

For civil purposes there was a 365-day count called, perhaps incorrectly, by some scholars the *haab*. It consisted of the elapsed days in eighteen named 20-day periods, called *uinals*, and in a supplementary 5-day period called *Uayeh*; these last were unlucky days. The *uinal* names were *Pop, Uo, Zip, ..., Kayab* and *Cumhu* (see Table 11.2). These days ran 0 *Pop*, 1 *Pop*, 2 *Pop*, 3 *Pop*, ..., 19 *Pop*, 0 *Uo*, 1 *Uo*, ..., 19 *Cumhu*, 0 *Uayeh*, 1 *Uayeh*, 2 *Uayeh*, 3 *Uayeh* and 4 *Uayeh*, the last being the 365th in the so-called *haab* series. This looks a little like the Egyptian civil year.

119

Pop	Yaxkin	Mac
Uo	Mol	Kankin
Zip	Chen	Muan
Zotz	Yax	Pax
Tzec	Zac	Kayab
Xul	Ceh	Cumhu

Table 11.2   The Yucatec names of the eighteen Mayan *uinals*. The period *Uayeh* of 5 unlucky days followed *Cumhu*.

The two series of pairs, one making up the *tzolkin* and the other the so-called *haab*, were taken together to give a double date as follows: 1 *Ik*, 0 *Pop*; 2 *Akbal*, 1 *Pop*; 2 *Kan*, 2 *Pop*; . . ., 12 *Ahau*, 18 *Mac*; 13 *Imix*, 19 *Mac* (last day of the *tzolkin*); 1 *Ik*, 0 *Kankin* (the first day of the next *tzolkin*); 2 *Akbal*, 1 *Kankin*; 3 *Kan*, 2 *Kankin*; . . ., 13 *Chicchan*, 3 *Uayeh*; 1 *Cimi*, 4 *Uayeh* (the last day of that *haab*); 2 *Manik*, 0 *Pop* (the first day of the next *haab*). Only after 18980 days (73 *tzolkins* or 52 *haabs* or about 51.69 tropical years) were all the possible unique double dates exhausted and both the *tzolkin* and the *haab* began again together on 1 *Ik* 0 *Pop*. This period is usually referred to as the Calendar Round. If one knew in what Calendar Round some double dated event occurred one thus knew the precise date on which it occurred.

In order to locate events within a longer period than 18980 days, the Maya took vigesimal multiples of a 360-day period (the *tun*). A *katun* was twenty *tuns* (or 7200 days), a *baktun* was twenty *katuns* (or 144000 days); for some purposes of calculation they also had the *pictun* (twenty *baktuns*), the *calabtun* (twenty *pictuns*), the *kinchiltun* (twenty *calabtuns*) and the *alautun* (twenty *kinchiltuns* or 23040000000 days or almost 63081 Julian years). In the Classic Period (fourth to ninth centuries AD), the Maya recorded on their monuments such dates as 9. 16. 0. 0. 0. 2 *Ahau* 13 *Tzec*, meaning that since the beginning of the Era in which they then placed themselves 9 *baktuns*, 16 *pictuns*, 0 *tun*, 0 *uinal* and 0 *kin* had elapsed, the day in question being 2 *Ahau* 13 *Tzec* in the Calendar Round then in progress. In our calendar the date just given was probably 27 October AD 751. The first day of the Era was taken to be 4 *Ahau* 8 *Cumbu*.

In the Classic Period certain additional information was given in the dates on monuments. First and most impressive was a correction for the discrepancy between the 365-day *haab* and the Mayan estimate of the tropical year (approximately 365.242 days) cumulated from the beginning of the Era. This was expressed as the number of days the double date, say 2 *Ahau* 13 *Tzac*, was ahead of the seasons in the *haab* in question as compared with its place at the beginning of the Era. The methods of calculating this correction cannot be explained simply but the interested reader may find a discussion of them in Appendix V of Thompson's monograph (1950). Second, an indication was given of the age of the Moon as an ordinal number in that lunar cycle in the year and the length (29 or 30 days) of that or perhaps of the preceding lunar cycle.

A great interest was also taken in the synodic period of Venus, averaging about 583.92 days but varying between about 581 and 587 days. The Maya took it to be a rounded 584 days (though they introduced a correction of a few days every now and then). Five Venus cycles of 584 days equal 2920 days which are equal to eight *haabs* of 365 days; further 65 Venus cycles equal 104 *haabs* and 146 *tzolkins* or 52 Calendar Rounds. It was by taking rounded numbers of days for different cyclical events, finding common multiples and then seeing how closely the events matched that the Maya overcame their ineptitude with fractions. After 50 Venus cycles of 584 days it would emerge on average that the observed heliacal rising of Venus was about 4 days ahead of its original date in the *haab*, so a needed correction of 4 days would be indicated.

It was in similar fashion that an indirect knowledge of the average length of the solar year and lunar synodic month was obtained, that is by matching multiples of lunations, of *haabs* and of eclipse intervals. In this way the Mayans estimated but could not express the fact in direct form that the tropical year was about 365.242 days and the lunar synodic month about 29.530864 days (see Thompson, 1950).

There is some evidence of a concern with other cycles, one perhaps being a Mercury cycle, but I have said enough to indicate the complexity and the ingenuity of Mayan calendrical and dating practices. Through simplifications in the dating practices, they lost in the post-Classic Period (ninth century AD to the arrival of the Spaniards) the precision they earlier possessed but the elaborate cycles interlocked with cycles continued. These calendrical schemes spread into Mexico to the Toltecs and later to the Aztecs. The names of days, of the 20-day periods (Maya *uinals*) and of the various counts changed, but numerically the complex scheme remained essentially unchanged.

I have drawn attention to the similarity of the Maya method of generating cycles of 260 *kin*, 365 *kin* and of 52 *haab* (the Calendar

Round) and the Chinese method of generating the sexagenary cycle; the resultant cycles, however, are quite different. Attention has been drawn to the similarity of the Mayan *haab* with its 360 days in the eighteen *uinals* plus the 5 unlucky days of *Uayeh* to the Egyptian civil year with its 360 days in the 12 schematic months plus the 5 epagomenal days. However, the Mayan *uinal* and the Egyptian schematic month are markedly different. The latter seems to be derived from the lunar months of 29 or 30 days of which the Maya had an accurate knowledge. The *uinal* may be based on man's twenty fingers and toes; at any rate the *Yucatec* word for man is *Uinic* or *Uinac*. I am sceptical about the suggestions that the Maya had been influenced by migrant Egyptians or migrant Chinese. I believe that there are more plausible explanations of the similarities in some respects of their calendrical practices to those of the ancient Egyptians and of the Chinese.

On numerous occasions above attention has been drawn to similarities and differences in calendrical and other time-reckoning practices amongst different cultures and regions. Sometimes there is clear enough external evidence of borrowing, a good example being the Zodiac. As there are alternative sets of astronomical markers, two calendar-makers may hit on the same or on different sets. In the former case they may go on quite independently to work out their systems showing remarkable correspondence in detail. Without external evidence that the Greeks, the Babylonians, the Indians and the Chinese borrowed one from another the Metonic Cycle, there is no inherent reason for assuming there must be borrowing. The same may be said about the Jupiter cycles. When, however, it comes to the arbitrary or conventional practices such as the twelve *beru* or the twenty-four hour division of the day, one has more justification in suspecting borrowing. Perhaps the seven-day week falls into the same class, though it could have been based on a rounding of the quarters of the Moon. The five epagomenal days of the Egyptians and of the Mayans are remainders from rounded estimates of the solar year (365 days) arrived at by such different processes, that without external evidence they are probably best regarded as coincidental parallels.

EPILOGUE

No calendar has been or ever will be perfect if it tries to fit the solar years and the lunar months together. There are additional difficulties if an attempt is made to fit in as well shorter arbitrary periods such as the week. Using whole days from wherever measured, only the weeks can come out neatly. If the lunar synodic months are nearly right, that is 29 and 30 days in rough alternation, the year must be wrong except on average. If the solar year is almost right, 365 days with 366 days about every fourth year, the months if treated as rough fractions of the year must be divorced from the phases of the Moon. Some calendars have done better than others. The pre-Julian Roman calendar got neither the months nor the years right even approximately. The Mohammedan calendar which gets the months approximately right has the years slipping rapidly through the seasons. The Egyptian civil calendar which broke away from the lunar months had a year which slipped forward slowly through the seasons. We have seen how complicated Hindu calendrical practices became in trying to observe the 7-day week, the lunar synodic month, the thirty 'lunar days' or *tithis*, the Sun's progress through the signs of the Zodiac and so on. Only a patient, resigned people like the Indians could bear to live with such a set of complexities. Their solar months must be praised as schematic divisions of the year, linked as they are with a natural event, the Sun's entry into the Signs.

There have been several instances of an older calendar being preserved for religious or other ceremonial purposes while some improved version has been in use for civil purposes. In our moderately good Gregorian calendar, we have the oddity of Christ's birthday being fixed (on a mistaken date for the Winter Solstice) and the days of his crucifixion and of his resurrection being movable, tied in approximate fashion to the first Sunday after the first full Moon after the Spring Equinox.

There have been various proposals in the twentieth century for a radical reform of the calendar. In general they aim to produce equal quarters of the year, 91 days, said to be for the convenience of those who calculate wages and interest on loans. This, of course, ignores the unequal seasons of the year. The proposed sets of 30, 30 and 31 day months ignore the phases of the Moon. In any case there is the extra named but dateless day in each year and a second roughly every 4 years on each of which interest and wages or holiday pay have to be paid. The modern electronic computer does not need exact uniformity of periods, so there is not much substance in this alleged advantage. The only advantage I can see in these proposed reforms is that they keep the day names and the dates in constant relation. Thus if 1 January occurs on a Monday, 1 February will be a Wednesday, 1 March a Friday, 1 April a Monday and so on, year after year. I doubt there is an advantage in this as it would be harder for me to memorize the dates and corresponding day-names than it is for me to consult my pocket diary.

The proposed reform which I have just described reminds me of the calendar proclaimed with varying degrees of precision in *Enoch* and *The Book of Jubilee*, two of the Apochrypha, and in at least one of the Dead Sea Scrolls (see Beckwith, 1970). Time-keeping by the Moon's phases was denounced and the year declared to be 364 days, made up of four quarters of 91 days each consisting of 30-, 30- and 31-day months. The only virtue of 364 days is that it contains exactly 52 weeks, periods of only conventional significance. At least that calendar had no monthless days and no days which were not days of the week. Were we to have unnumbered days outside the named months I can imagine them becoming unlucky days, despite names such as World Day and Leap Year Day, and that parents would become inclined, as did the Maya in respect of *Uayeh* days, to delay the announcement of the birth of children unfortunate enough to be born on a dateless, monthless day.

Neugebauer (1969) speaking of the Egyptian civil calendar with its invariant 365-day year said 'This calendar is, indeed, the only intelligent calendar which existed in human history'. Its operation over so long a span of time, about three millennia, and the constancy of its years made it attractive to Hellenistic, medieval and early modern astronomers. The interval between two astronomical events dated reliably in terms of it could be worked out exactly to the day. The pre-Julian Roman calendar with its irregularly (perhaps whimsically would be the better word) intercalated months was quite useless for such a purpose. Even after the Babylonians standardized the placing of an embolistic year in the nineteen-year (Metonic) cycle, their calendar was not as useful for these purposes without a preserved record showing which months were 29 and which 30 days; the same may be said of the Chinese calendar, especially as it was 'reformed' slightly from time to time. I shall forbear from commenting in this context on the almost bewilderingly complex later Indian calendar set.

The advantage given to astronomers by the Egyptian civil calendar was also provided by the Julian calendar (except in that period after Julius' assassination when the pontifices were intercalating a day too frequently) and by the slightly variant form of it introduced by Pope Gregory. It is true that the arithmetic is a little more complicated. One must identify which years have 366 days and allow for the extra day—a task I found not beyond me when I was using Popper's (1955) data.

I am far from certain that 'intelligent' is the right word for a calendar which had the year of the seasons slip backwards through it in about 1500 years. 'Rational' as contrasted with 'empirical' would seem more appropriate. It was certainly not the only rational calendar in human history. The 364-day calendar in Palestine in the late first millennium BC is equally rational, though it has the disadvantage of few dates, if any, being given in terms of it and of its use for only a few hundred years. A better claim may be made for the Meso-American calendar with its *tzolkin* of 260 days, its so-called *haab* of 365 days and its Calendar Round of 18980 days, with double dates in both the *tzolkin* and the *haab*. Thus in addition to questioning Neugebauer's 'intelligent', I question his 'only' as applied to the Egyptian calendar.

In times when we English-speakers are going metric, that is, decimal-izing our currency, if it was not already in decimal form, and our weights and measures of length, area, volume, pressure, etc., it is a wonder that some addict in authority has not been moved to foist a decimalized time scale on us. In the areas where the switch to a decimal system has been or is planned to be effected the units are arbitrary even if tied to some empirical bench mark(s) such as the freezing and boiling points of water at average sea-level atmospheric pressure. Though it may be more convenient to call these two bench marks of temperature 0°C and 100°C respectively rather than 32°F and 212°F, for most, if not all, purposes it does not matter much to us what we call them so long as we have uniformity of convention. Other things, just about as important to us as water, freeze and boil at other points in the scale and we are concerned with the freezing and boiling of water at altitudes other than sea-level.

125

It is very hard, however, not to take notice of days and of tropical years, even though for convenience we schematize them a little. As the tropical year is not a neat multiple of either true or mean solar days we resort to the scheme of ordinary years with 365 days and leap years with 366 days. But this does not yield a neat decimal multiple. This is where the rub is.

The fractions into which we divide the day are arbitrary and we could quite readily and with only the initial inconvenience of accommodation to a new system use decimal fractions, tenths (2 hours 24 minutes), hundredths (14 minutes 24 seconds), thousandths (1 minute 26.4 seconds), ten thousandths (8.64 seconds) of a mean solar day, and so on. We could replace our 7-day week, which is quite arbitrary, with a *decadies* of 10 days, working perhaps 4 days and resting 1 and so having in effect a 5-day *semi-decadies*. Three such *decadies* or decades would be roughly equal to a month but the preservation of the month would not be in the true decimal spirit. For that matter the Australian 2 cent coin and 2 dollar note and the British $2\frac{1}{2}$ pence coin are not in the true decimal spirit. I see no point in the hundred-day multiple and no decimal multiple of days will yield a tropical year which I believe we need to preserve, at least in its present approximate form.

We have in the West abandoned the approximate lunar synodic month though the Mohammedans have preserved it, as have the Jews for religious purposes and the Indians with the *chandra masa* in their complex calendar. We have learned to live with only vestigial months not tied to the cycles of the Moon. Indeed, urbanized society thinks of full Moons only on occasions of electric power crises. I would not object to a slight variation in the number of days in our months so that sets of three of them were a little nearer to the intervals, to the nearest whole day, between equinoxes and solstices, but I do not advocate such a change. I can also see some sense in starting the year on the day within which some chosen equinox or solstice occurs but again I do not advocate the possibility.

We are used to decades and centuries of years and to millennia but I believe that we would find tenths of a year (36.52422 days, or 36 days 12 hours 34 minutes and 52.61 seconds), hundredths (3.652422 days or 3 days 15 hours 39 minutes and 29.26 seconds), thousandths (0.3652422 days or 8 hours 45 minutes 56.93 seconds) of no practical use in themselves. We might learn to live with the smaller fractions though none of them are neat fractions of the solar day which is so important to us in our round of work, recreation and rest.

Therefore somewhat in the spirit of the cry 'Give us back our eleven days' uttered by the rioting crowds in Britain in 1752, let me make a plea to keep our seconds, minutes, hours, days, weeks, months and years, strange historical hodge-podge though the whole system be. It was meant to help us reckon the passage of time and it does. There are many other things in more urgent need of reform.

In the so-called Christian world, there would be advantages in changing the movable feasts based on Easter to fixed dates in our irrational calendar.

APPENDIX

DAY NAMES IN VARIOUS LANGUAGES

Some hints of the mixed origins of the 7-day week which so many communities now observe may be found in the names of the days used in a number of modern languages. I shall give first the Latin names used in early Imperial Roman times and then give some more recent names set out under related language groups.

LATIN   *Dies Solis, Dies Lunae, Dies Martis, Dies Mercurii, Dies Iouis, Dies Veneris, Dies Saturni*

Romance Languages

ITALIAN   *Domenica, Lunedi, Martedi, Mercoledi, Giovedi, Venerdi, Sabato*
FRENCH   *dimanche, lundi, mardi, mercredi, jeudi, vendredi, samedi*
SPANISH   *el domingo, el lunes, el martes, el merceles, el jeuves, el viernes, el sabado*
PORTUGUESE   *domingo, segunda-fiera, tercia-fiera, quarta-fiera, quinta-fiera, sexta-fiera, sabado*

Notes

1. There is a clear tendency in these languages as in Byzantine and Modern Greek (*Kyriaki*) to convert *Dies Solis*, the Sun's day, into the Lord's day. Granted that *Dies Saturni* or *Shabbat* was the day before Christ's resurrection, this is not surprising. Perhaps there is a similar relation between Christmas Day and the third century Roman *Dies Natalis Solis Invicti*, a conventional if not accurate day of the Winter Solstice.
2. The Jewish *Shabbat* is clearly reflected in *Sabato*, etc. I shall offer a comment on the French *samedi* later.
3. The Portuguese day names follow Eastern rather than Western church practice.

MODERN GREEK   *Kyriaki, deutera, triti, tetarti, pempti, paraskeni* and *sabbaton*.
Notes

1. These words mean Lord's (day), second (day), third (day), ... preparation (for the Sabbath) and Sabbath.
2. In some Greek dialects *sabbaton* is *sambaton* which may be the source of the French *samedi* and the German *Samstag*. It may be worth remembering that

the ancient Egyptian equivalent of the Akkadian *sabbatu*, full Moon, was *smdt*.

3. Though the planetary names were scratched on the walls of Pompeii in Greek as well as in Latin, the Eastern Church seems not to have adopted them.

Teutonic Languages

GERMAN   *Sonntag, Montag, Dienstag, Mittwoch, Donnerstag, Freitag, Samstag* (or *Sonnabend*)

DUTCH   *Zondag, Maandag, Dinsdag, Woensdag, Dondersdag, Vrejdag, Zaterdag*

SWEDISH   *sondag, mandag, tisdag, onsdag, torsdag, fredag, lordag*

OLD ENGLISH   *Sunnandaeg, Monandaeg, Tiwesdaeg, Wodnesdaeg, Thuresdaeg, Frigedaeg, Saeternesdaeg*

Notes

1. Danish and Norwegian and Icelandic day-names are essentially the same as Swedish.
2. Old English, English, Dutch, the Scandinavian languages and German to varying extents substitute Twia for Mars, Woden for Mercury, Thor for Jupiter and Fria for Venus in the planetary scheme.
3. Dutch and German have a day of service, to whom I am not sure, for Mars' or Twia's day.
4. The German *Mittwoch* (mid-week) for Woden's day is parallelled in a number of Slavic languages.
5. Only Dutch, Old English and Modern English preserve Saturn's day; *Samstag* as already stated may be related to *Sambaton*, the Greek dialectal variant; *Sonnabend* is the eve of Sunday; and *lordag* is bath-day, or more literally soap-day.

Slavic Languages

RUSSIAN   *woskresienje, poniedielnik, wotornik, sreda, czetwierg, piatnica, subbota*

POLISH   *niedziela, poniedzialek, wtorek, sroda, czwartek, piatek, sobota*

Notes

1. *Niedziela* the Polish name for Sunday, and cognate words in most other Slavic languages, means 'no activity'. *Poniedielnik* in Russian and its cognates mean 'after no activity'. The Russian *woskresienje*, and there is a similar word in Ukrainian, means 'resurrection'.
2. *Sreda, sroda* and their cognates in other Slavic languages mean 'middle', akin to the German *Mittwoch*.
3. *Subbota, sobota* and their cognates are obviously from *sabbaton*.
4. The other day names mean 'second', 'fourth' and 'fifth' respectively, thus making *poniedzialek* (Monday) the first day of the week.

Sanskrit

Shortly after the time when the planetary day names were officially adopted by the Emperor Constantine, they came into use in India translated into Sanskrit, most probably as part of a lot of other Hellenistic Greek astronomical and astrological nomenclature. The series were

ravivara, somavara, mangalavara, saumyavara,

brihaspativara, sukravara and *sanivara.*

The suffix, *vara*, is day and the stems are the names of the Sun (there were alternatives such as *Sura*), the Moon (the more usual was *Candra* but the Moon was also likened to a drop of *soma*, a ceremonially used intoxicating drink) and the planets Mars, Mercury, Jupiter, Venus and Saturn.

SELECT BIBLIOGRAPHY

Achelis, E., *The Calendar for Everybody*, Putnam, New York 1943.

——, *Of Time and the Calendar*, Heritage, New York 1955.

Allen, R. H., *Star-names and their Meanings*, Stechert, New York 1899.

Ashbrook, J., 'Some very thin lunar crescents', *Sky and Telescope*. 42 1971, 2, pp. 78–9.

——, 'More about the visibility of the lunar crescent', *Sky and Telescope*, 43 1972, 2, pp. 95–6.

Beckwith, R. T., 'The modern attempt to reconcile the Qumran calendar with the true solar year', *Revue de Qumran*, 7 1970, 27, pp. 379–96.

Bede, the Venerable, *De temporibus*, Vol. VI *Complete Works*, J. A. Giles (ed.), Whittaker, London 1893.

——, *The Ecclesiastical History of the English Nation*, trans. by M. Maclagan, Blackwell, Oxford 1949.

Bickerman, E. J., *Chronology of the Ancient World*, Thames and Hudson, London 1968.

Boll, F., *Sphaera*, Teubner, Leipzig 1903. Facsimile reprint, Georg Olms, Hildersheim 1967.

Boll, F. and Gundel, W., 'Sternbilder, Sternglauke and Sternsymbolik bei Greichen und Römern'. In W. H. Roscher (ed.), *Ausführliches Lexikon der greichischen und römischen Mythologie*, Vol. 6, 1937.

Censorinus, *De die natali liber*, O. Jahn (ed.), Georg Olms, Hildesheim 1965.

Chu Wen-Isin, *Li-fa-thung-chih*, 1934. (Not sighted; data generously extracted for me by Professor Ho Peng-yoke.)

Colson, F. H., *'The Week: an essay on the origin and development of the seven-day cycle;* Cambridge University Press, London 1926.

Cumont, F. V. M., *Astrology and Religion among the Greeks and Romans*, Putnam, New York 1912.

de Saussure, L., 'Le zodiaque lunaire asiatique', *Arch. des sciences physiques et naturelles*, 1, 1919a, pp. 105–26.

——, 'Le systeme astronomique des chinois', *Arch. des sciences physiques et naturelles*, 1, 1919b and 1920, pp. 186–216, pp. 561–88; 2, pp. 214–31, pp. 325–50.

——, 'Origine babylonienne de l'astronomie chinoise', *Arch. des sciences physiques et naturelles*, 5, 1923, pp. 5–18.

Dio Cassius, *Roman History*, trans. by Earnest Cary, Heinemann, London. 1st imp. 1914, rep. 1954.

Dreyer, J. L. E., *A History of Astronomy from Thales to Kepler*, (formerly *A History of Planetary Systems from Thales to Kepler*, 1905), Dover Publications, New York 1953.

Encyclopaedia Britannica, article 'Calendar' in Vol 4, 1973, pp. 611–28.

Encyclopaedia of Religion and Ethics, J. Hastings (ed.), article 'Calendar' in Vol. 3, pp. 61–141, Clark, Edinburgh 1910.

Fotheringham, J. K., 'The Calendar' in *The Nautical Almanac for the Year* 1931, HMSO, London 1930.

Fowler, W. Warde, *The Roman Festivals of the Period of the Republic,* Macmillan, London 1899.

Gardiner, A. H., *Egyptian Grammar,* Clarendon Press, Oxford 1927.

Góssmann, F., *Planatarium Babylonicum,* Band 2, Teil IV of A. Deimel's *Sumerisches Lexikon,* Papstal, Bibelinstituts 1950.

Hartner, W., 'The earliest history of the constellations and the motif of the lion-bull combat', *J. Near Eastern Studies,* Vol. 24, 1965, pp. 1–16, + plates.

Hesiod, *'Works and Days',* English trans. by H. G. Evelyn-White, in *The Homeric Hymns and Homerica.* Heinemann, London 1967.

Hsueh Chung-san and Ou-yang, I., *A Sino-European Calendar for Two Thousand Years:* 1-2000 A.D., (place and publisher not detectable), 1955.

King, L. W., *Babylonian Boundary-stones and Memorial-tablets,* British Museum, London 1912.

Jones, A. H. M., *Constantine and the Conversion of Europe,* English Universities Press, London 1949.

Langdon, S., *The Babylonian Epic of Creation,* Clarendon Press, Oxford 1923.

——, *Babylonian menologies and the Semitic Calendars,* Oxford University Press, London 1935.

MacDonell, A. A., *A Practical Sanskrit Dictionary,* Oxford University Press, London 1954.

Macrobius, *The Saturnalia,* trans. by P. V. Davies, Columbia University Press, New York 1969.

Maspero, G., *Manual of Egyptian Archaeology,* 5th edn, H. Grevel & Co., London 1914.

Meritt, B. D., *The Athenian Year,* University of California Press, 1961.

Meissner, B., (bearbeitet von W. von Soden), *Akkadisches Handwörterbuch,* Otto Harrassowitz, Wiesbaden 1965.

Michels, A., *The Calendar of the Roman Republic,* Princeton University Press, 1967.

Morley, S. G. and Brainerd G. W., *The Ancient Maya,* Stanford University Press, 1963.

Needham, J., *Science and Civilisation in China,* Vol. 3. Cambridge University Press, London 1959.

Neugebauer, O., 'The origin of the Egyptian calendar', *J. Near Eastern Studies,* Vol. 1, (1942) pp. 396–403.

——, 'The history of ancient astronomy: problems and methods', *J. Near Eastern Studies*, 4, (1945), pp. 1–38.

——, 'The water clock in Babylonian astronomy,' *Isis*, 37, 1947, pp. 37–43.

——, 'The alleged Babylonian discovery of the precession of the equinoxes', *J. Amer. Oriental Society*, 70, 1950, pp. 1–8.

——, *The Exact Sciences in Antiquity*. Dover Publications, New York 1969. (A slightly revised version of the second edition published by Brown Univeristy Press, 1957).

Neugebauer, O. and Parker, R. A., *Egyptian Astronomical Texts*, Vol. I, Brown University Press, Providence, Rhode Island, 1960.

Neugebauer, O. and Pritchett, W. K., *The Calendars of Athens,* Cambridge, Mass. 1947.

Newton, R. R., *Medieval Chronicles and the Rotation of the Earth,* Johns Hopkins University Press, Baltimore and London 1942.

Norton, A. P. and Gall Inglis, J., *Norton's Star Atlas and Reference Book*. Gall and Inglis, London 1957. (The first edition by Norton was published in 1910).

Pannekoek, A., *A History of Astronomy*, Interscience Publishers, New York 1961. (Trans. from *De Groei van on Wereldbeeld*. Wereld-Bibliotheek, Amsterdam 1951).

Parker, R. A., *The Calendars of Ancient Egypt,* Chicago University Press, Chicago 1950.

Parker, R. A. and Dubberstein W. A., *Babylonian Chronology*, 626 *B.C.–A.D.* 75, Brown University Press, Providence 1956.

Payne-Gaposchkin, C., *Introduction to Astronomy,* Methuen, London 1961. (Previously published in the U.S.A., 1954).

Plutarch. *Lives,* trans. by Bernadotte Perrin, Heinemann, London, 1st pr. 1914, rep. 1959.

Poole, R. L. 'The beginning of the year in the Middle Ages' in *Studies in Chronology and History*, Clarendon Press, Oxford 1969, pp. 1–27.

Popper, W. *The Cairo Nilometer*, University of California Press, California 1951.

Powell, T. G. E., *The Celts*, Thames and Hudson, London 1958.

Pritchett, W. K., *Ancient Athenian Calendars on Stone,* University of California Publications in Classical Archaeology, 4, 1963, No. 4, pp. 267–402.

Renou, L. and Filliozat J., *L'Indique classique: manuel des Estudes Indiennes,* Vol. II, Imprimerie Nationale, Paris 1953.

Richmond, B., *Time Measurement and Calendar Construction,* Brill, Leiden 1956.

Sachs, A., 'Babylonian horoscopes', *J. Cuneiform Studies*, 6, 1952a, pp. 49–75.

——, 'Sirius dates in Babylonian astronomical texts of the Seleucid period', *J. Cuneiform Studies*, 6, 1952b, pp. 105–14.

Samuel, A. E., *Greek and Roman Chronology*, Bech'sche Verlagsbuchhandlung, München 1972.

Schoch, C., 'Astronomical and calendarial tables' in S. Langdon and J. K. Fotheringham, *The Venus Tables of Ammizaduga*, Oxford University Press, London 1928.

Sewell, R., *Indian Chronography*, Allen and Unwin, London 1912.

——, *The Siddhantas and the Indian Calendar*, Government of India Central Publication Branch, Calcutta 1924.

Sewell, R. and Dikshit, S. B., *The Indian Calendar*, Swan Sonneschein, London 1896.

Sivin, N., *Cosmos and Computation in Early Chinese Mathematical Astronomy*, Brill, Leiden 1969.

Skeat, W. W., (ed.), *G. Chaucer's A Treatise on the Astrolabe*, Trubner, London 1872.

Spencer Jones, H., *General Astronomy*, Edward Arnold, 2nd edn, London 1934.

The Flammarion Book of Astronomy, Allen and Unwin, London 1964. An English translation by Annabel and Bernard Pagel of a revision of Camille Flammarion's *Astronomie populaire* carried out under the direction of Gabrielle Camille Flammarion and Andre Danjon.

The Indian Ephemeris and Nautical Almanac for the year 1967, Government of India Press, Calcutta.

Thompson, J. E. S., *Maya Hieroglyphic Writing: Introduction*, Carnegie Institution Publication 589, Washington D. C. 1950.

Tuckerman, B., *Planetary, Lunar & Solar Positions*, Vol. I, 601 BC to AD 1. Vol. II, AD 2 to AD 1649. Amer. Philos. Soc., Philadelphia 1962, 1964.

Ungnad, A., 'Besprechungskunst und Astrologie in Babylonien', *Archiv für Orientforschung*, 14, 1941–4, pp. 251–84.

van der Waerden, B. L., 'The thirty-six stars', *J. Near Eastern Studies*, 8, 1949, pp. 6–26.

——, 'History of the zodiac', *Archiv für Orientforschung*, 16, 1953, pp. 218–30.

Varro, Marcus Terentius, *De lingua Latina*, trans. by R. G. Kent, Heinemann, London 1958.

Webster, H., *Rest Days: A Study in Early Law and Morality*, Macmillan, New York 1916.

Winlock, H. E., 'The origin of the ancient Egyptian calendar, *Proc. Amer. Philos. Soc.*, 83, 1940, pp. 447–64.

Wood, H., *Unveiling the Universe*, Angus and Robertson, Sydney 1967.

INDEX